I dedicate this book first to God, my source of inspiration and guide in all the journeys of my life. May your wisdom be the source of my eternal knowledge.
To my family who have always been by my side, supporting me and encouraging my goals. To you, I dedicate this book with all my love and affection.

Flávio Oliveira
2024

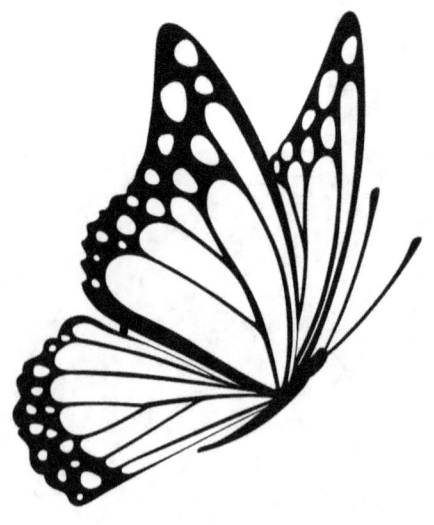
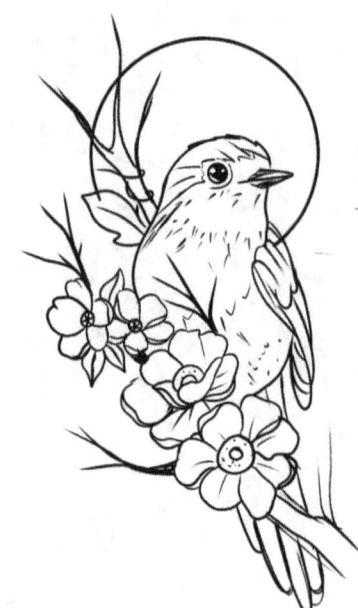

# This Book Belongs to:

_____

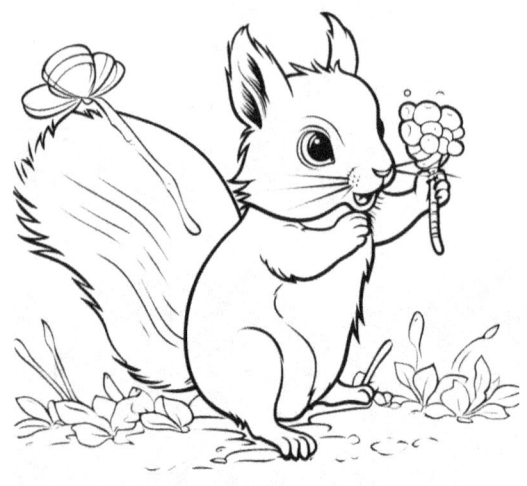
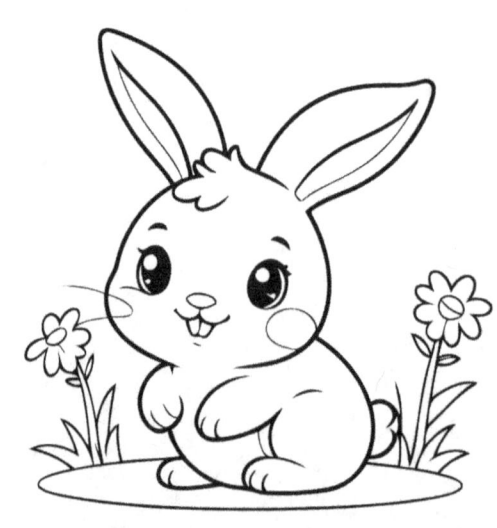

F.A. Oliveira©
all rights reserved

# ALL RIGHTS RESERVED©
## 2024

No part of this publication may be reproduced, distributed, or transmitted in any form or by any means, including photocopying, recording, or other electronic or mechanical methods, without the prior written permission of the publisher, except for brief quotations incorporated in critical reviews and other specific noncommercial uses. Any unauthorized replica of this work is prohibited.

F.A. Oliveira©

# Test Color Page

**Once upon a time, there was a beautiful little kitten named Mimo who loved his little house and lived next to an enchanted forest full of cute animals.**

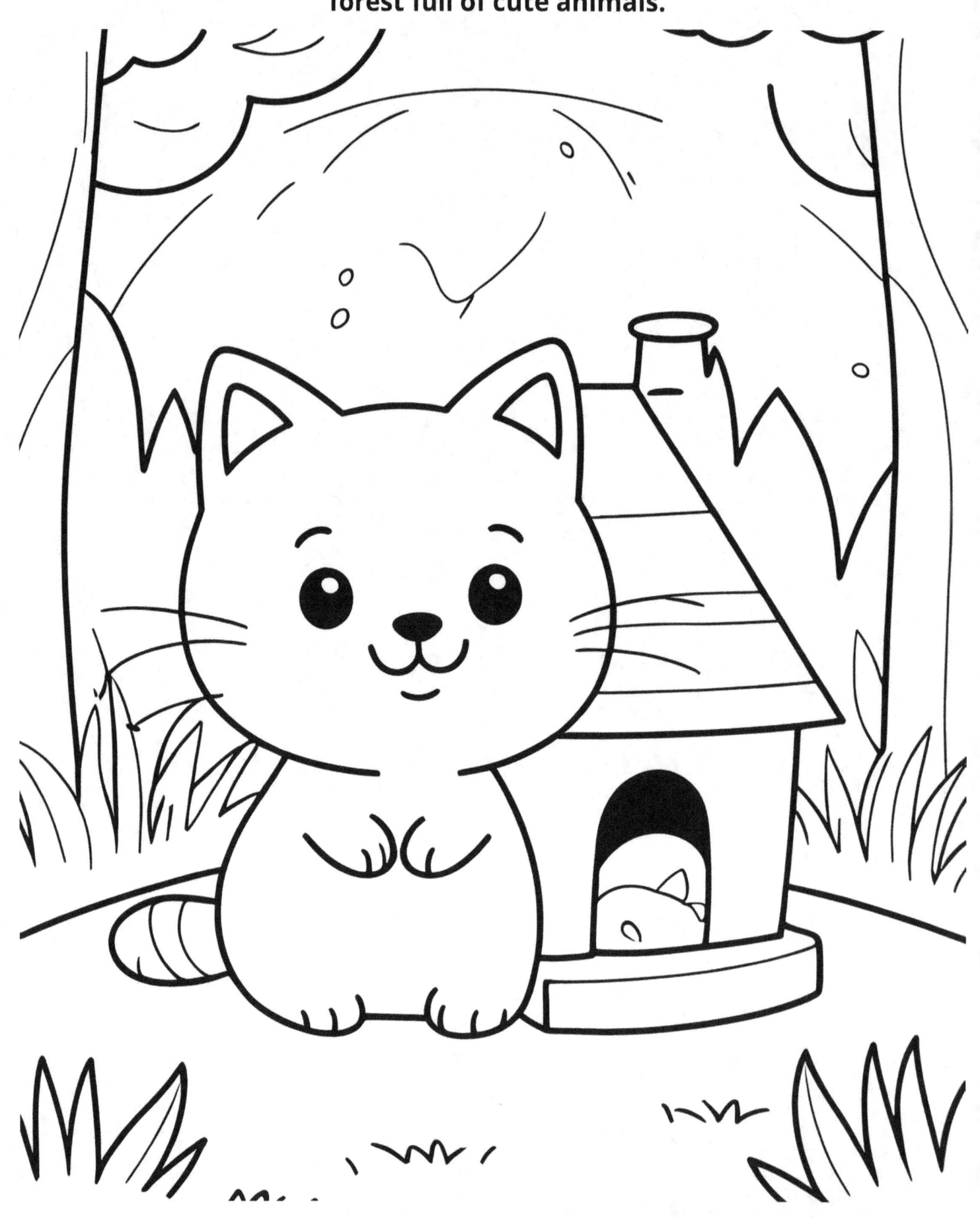

**On a beautiful sunny morning, Mimo the kitten decided to explore the forest. His eyes sparkled as he began his exploration into the unknown**

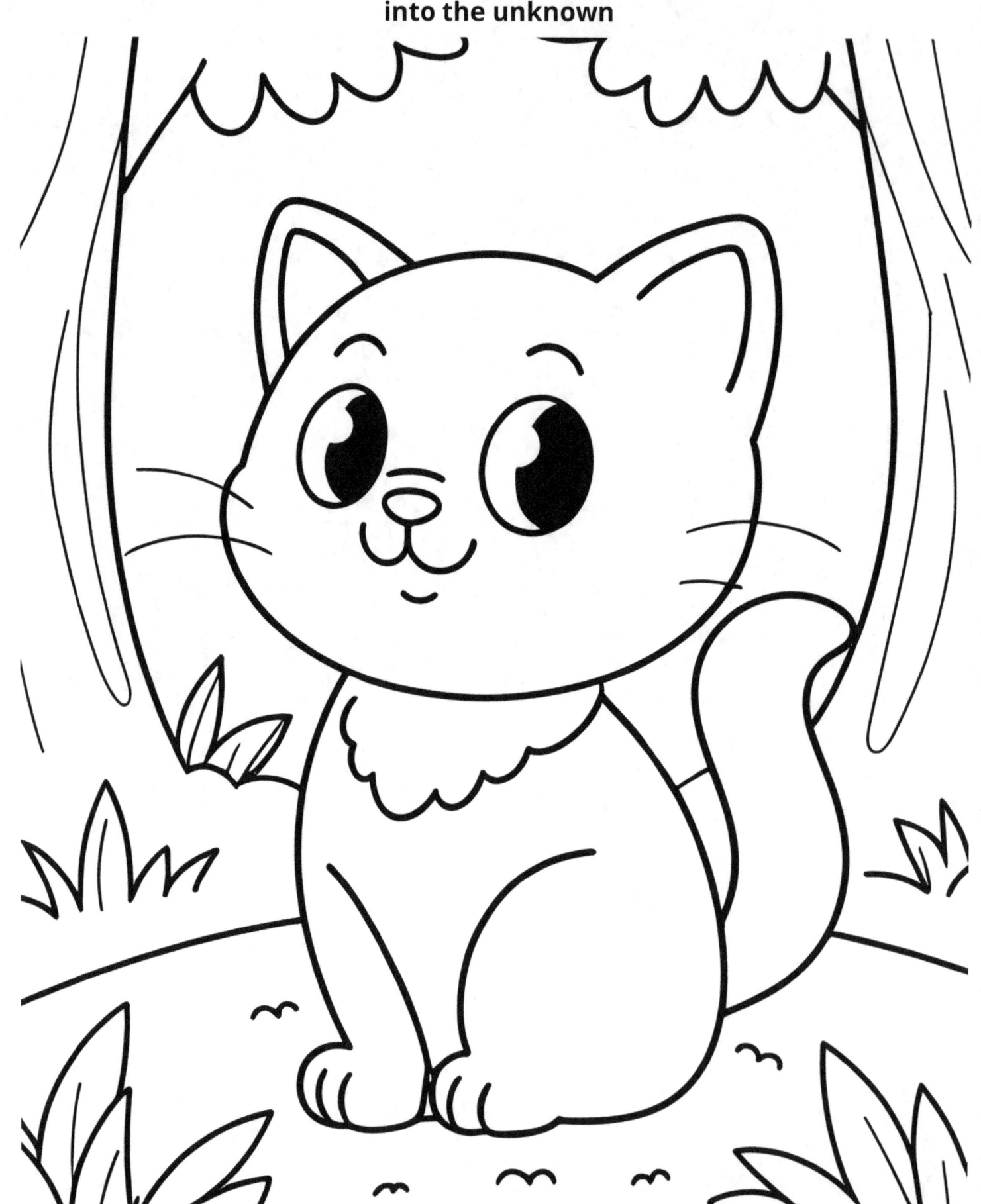

**While walking quietly through the woods, Mimo spotted a cute bunny bouncing around and shouted, "Hello little friend!" The little rabbit stopped and waved his little ears.**

**Together, they continued walking and having fun every moment in their adventure through the enchanted forest.**

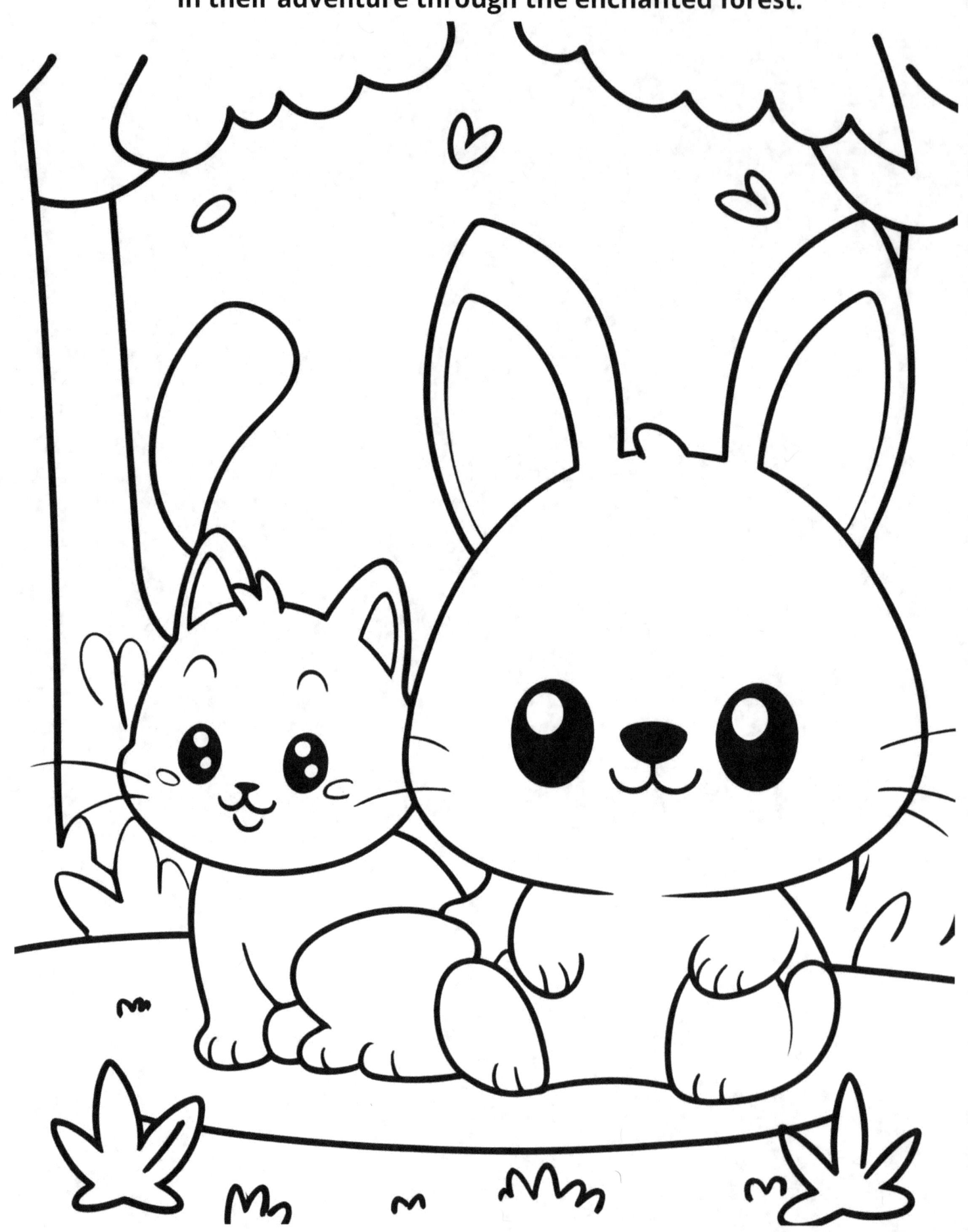

**Mimo and the bunny find three squirrels in a tree. They were very happy with the meeting and, more than quickly, they joined their new friends.**

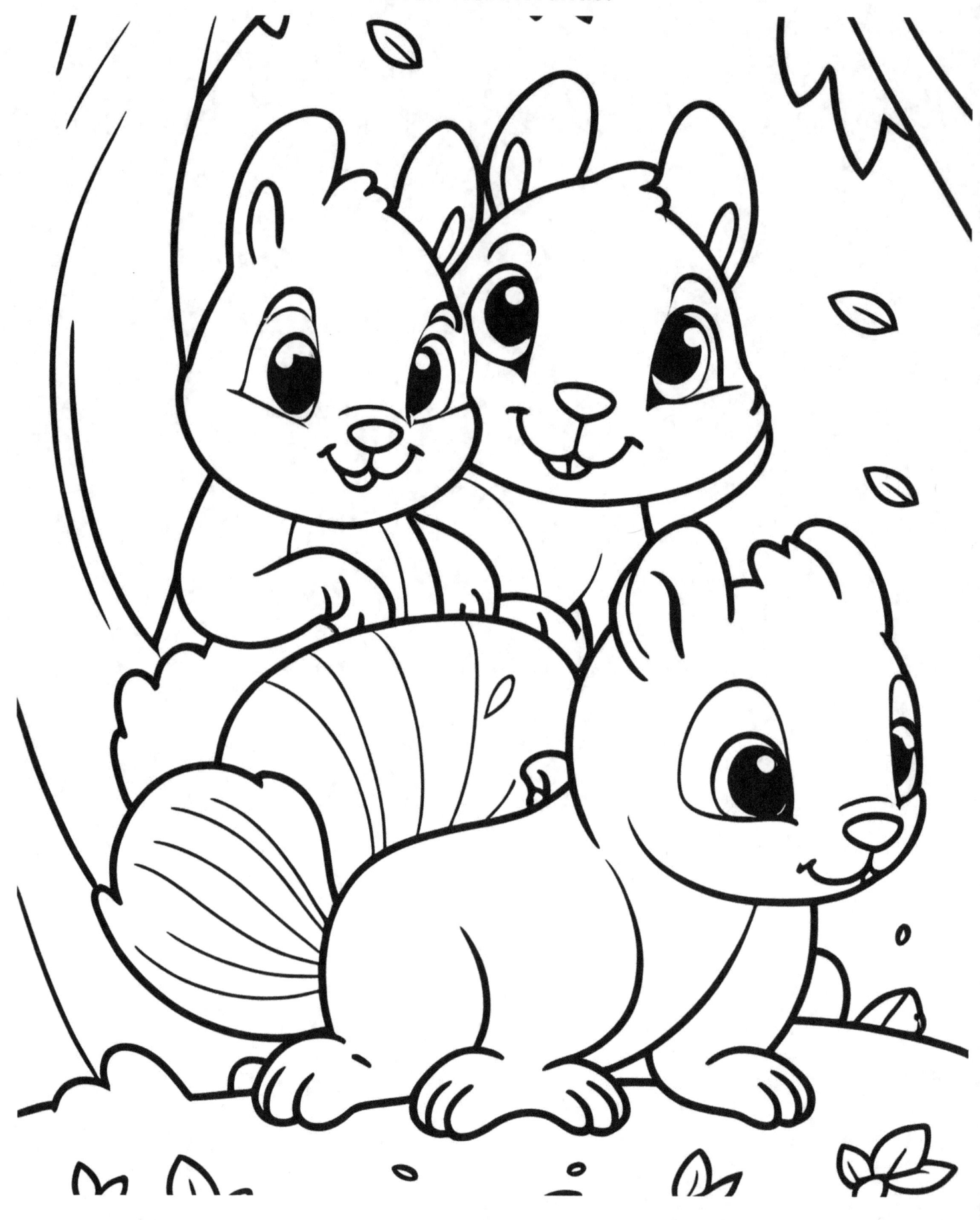

**One of the squirrels who was named Fluffy was very hungry. He had picked some nuts and was eating them to satisfy his hunger.**

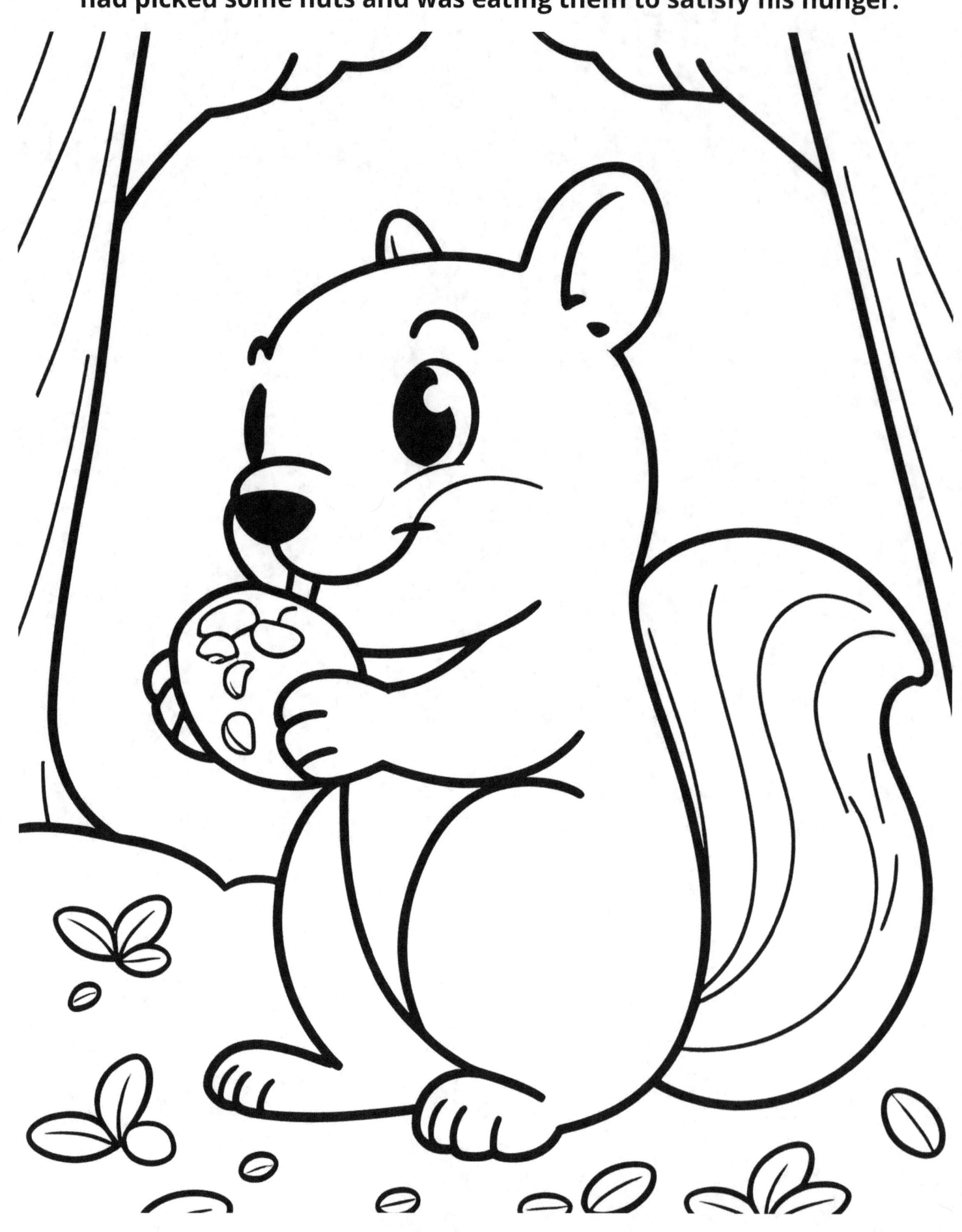

**The kitten, very happy with his adventure, looked up and was surprised. "How beautiful."**

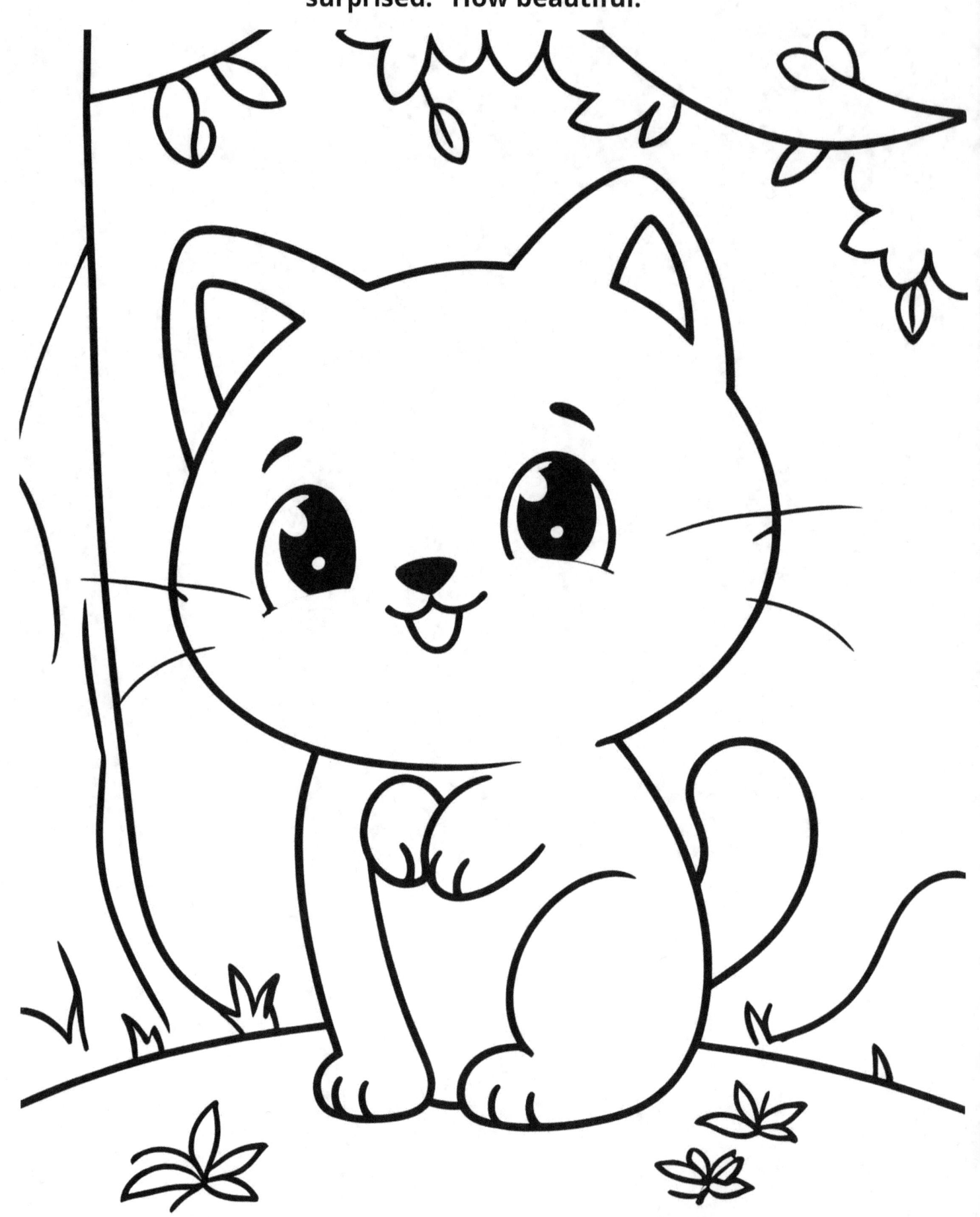

**It was a beautiful bird!**

**Mimo's happiness was enormous, and his heart throbbed with excitement at his adventure through the forest. He found other pets, but he didn't know their names. Do you know these animals?**

_____

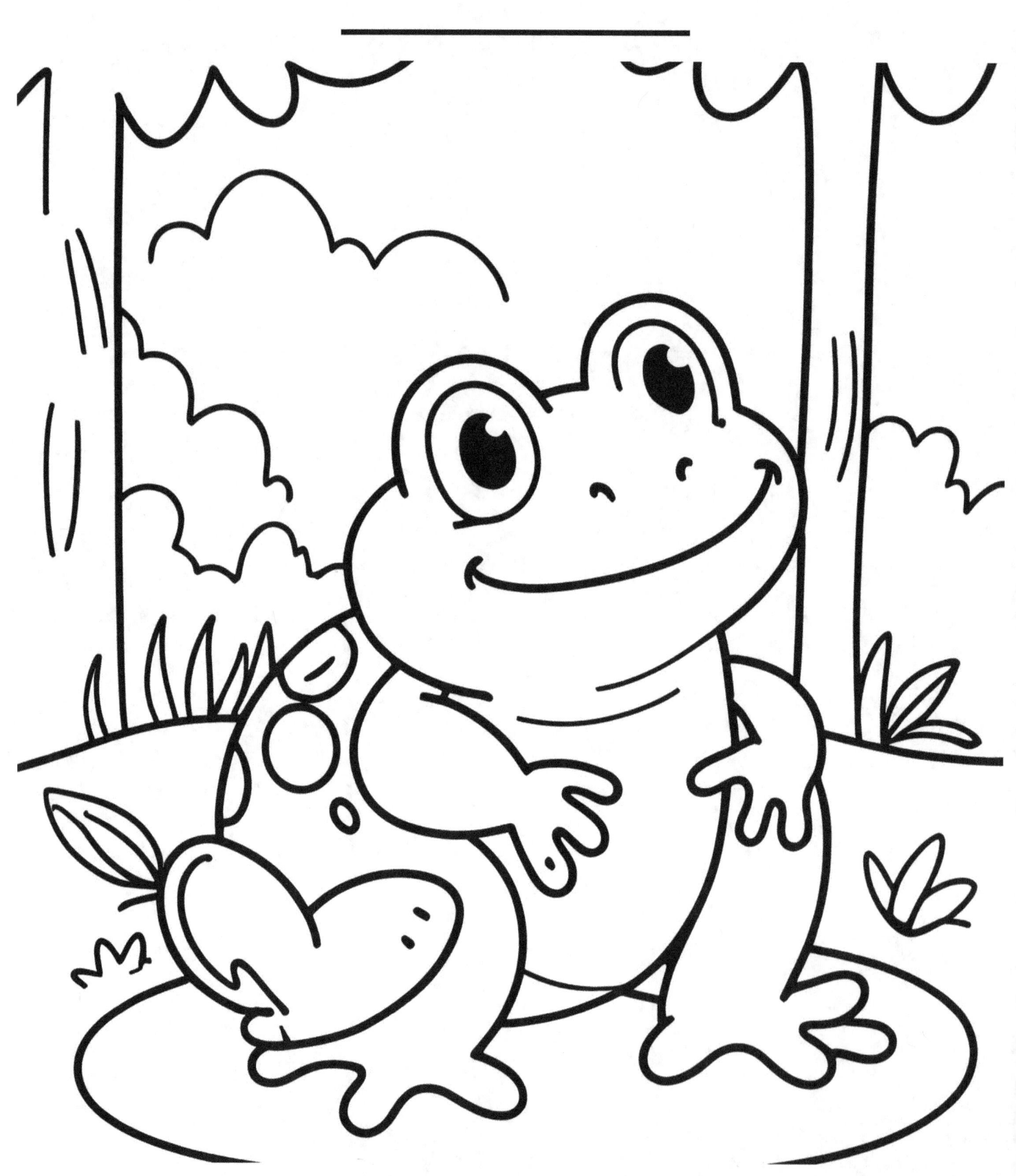

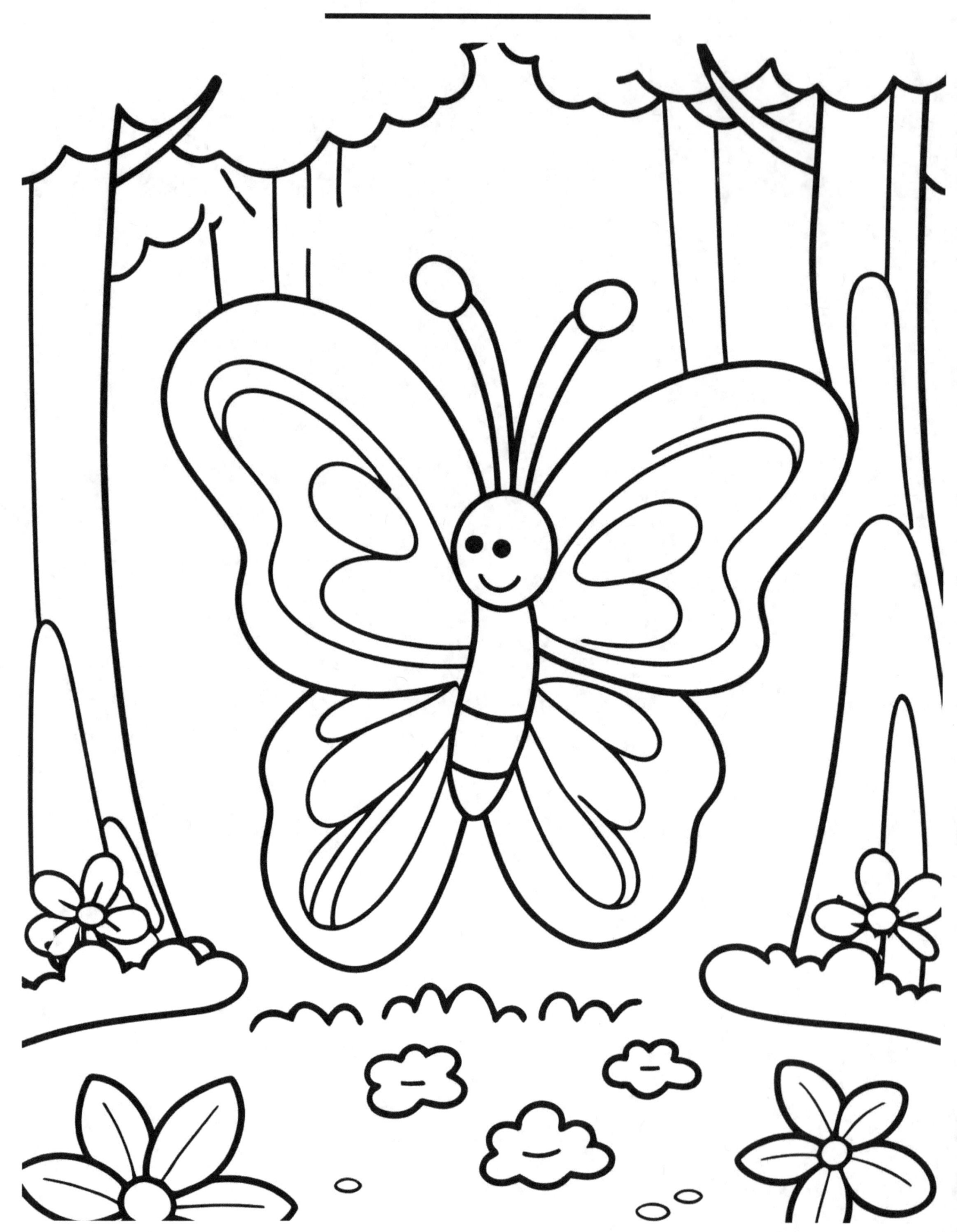

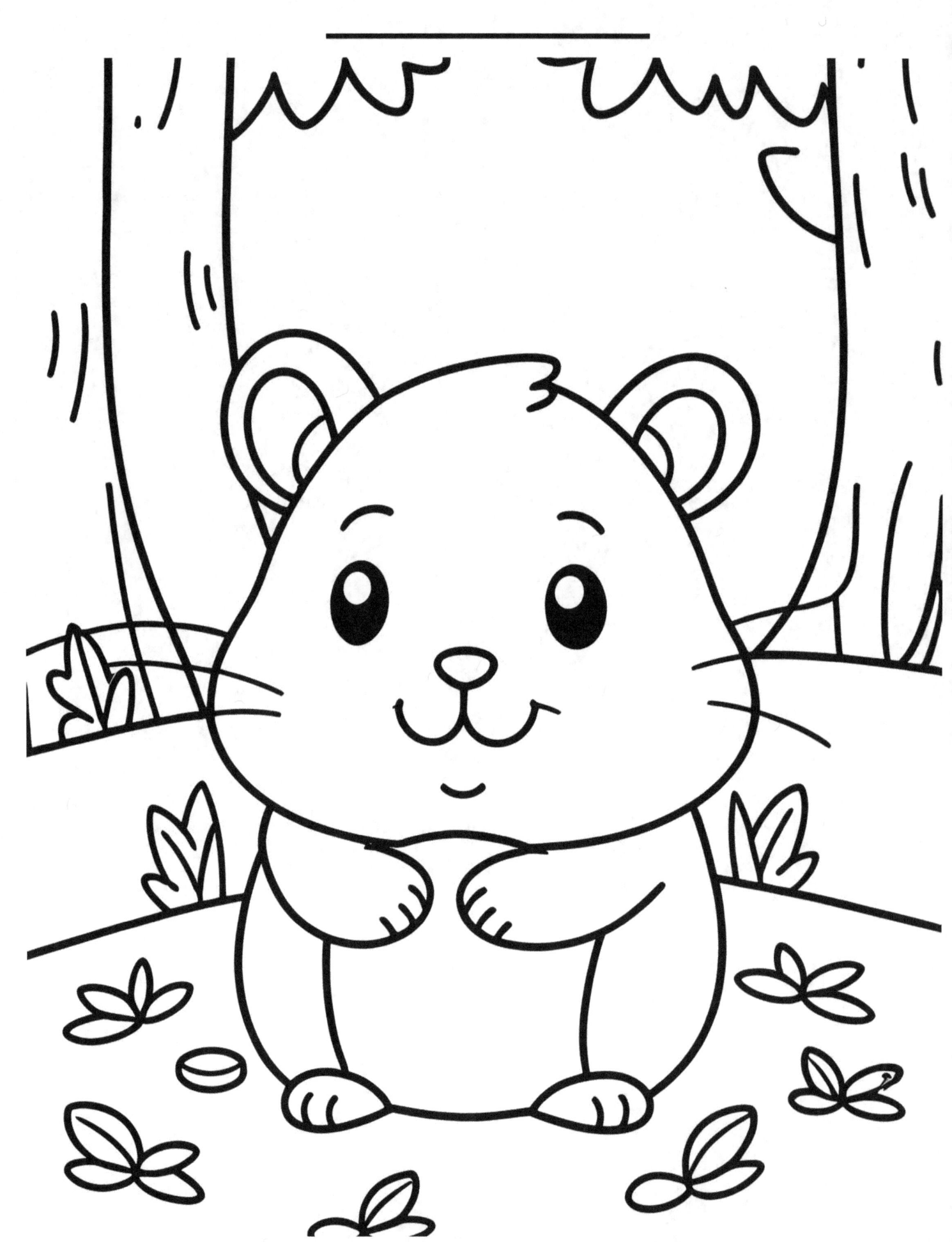

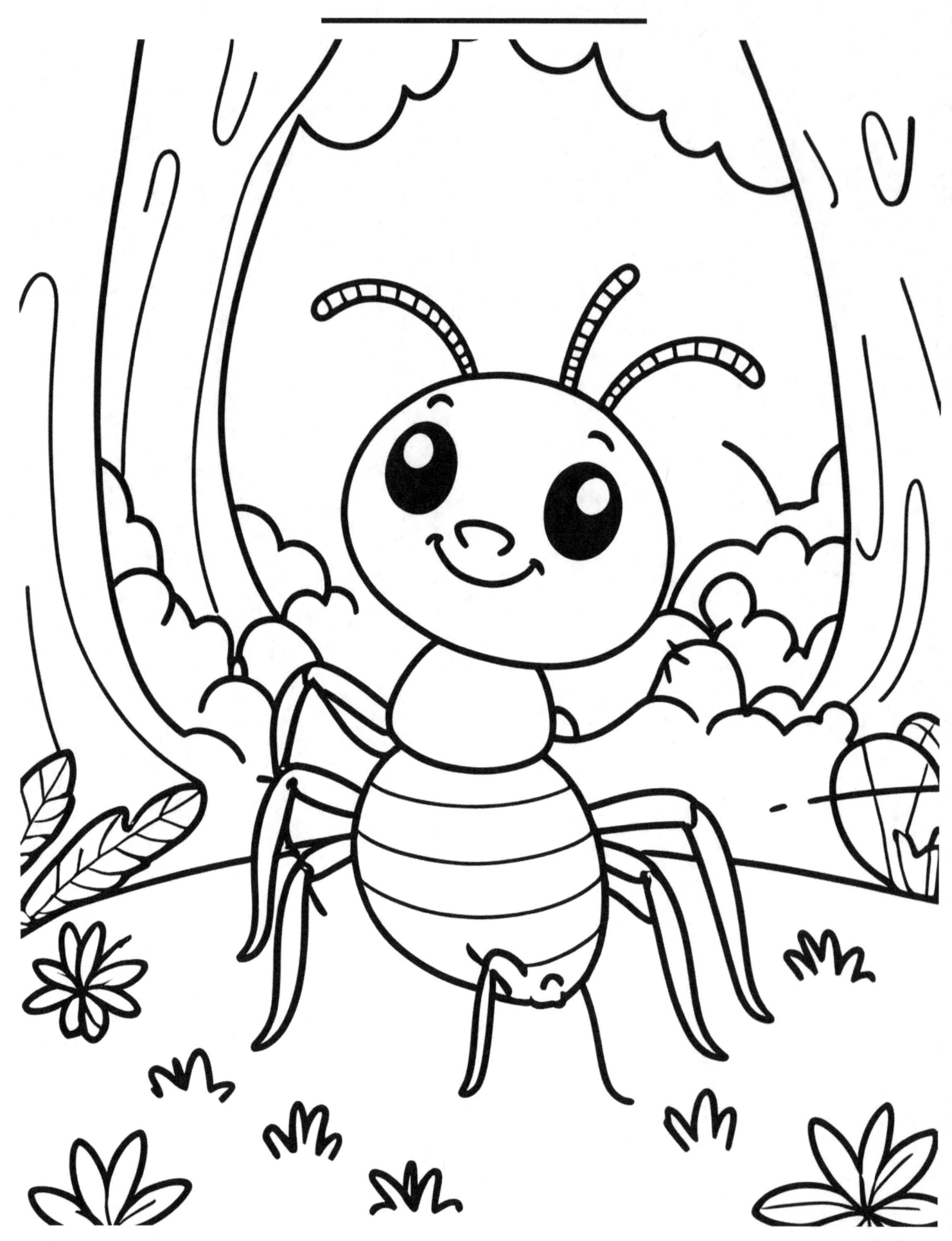

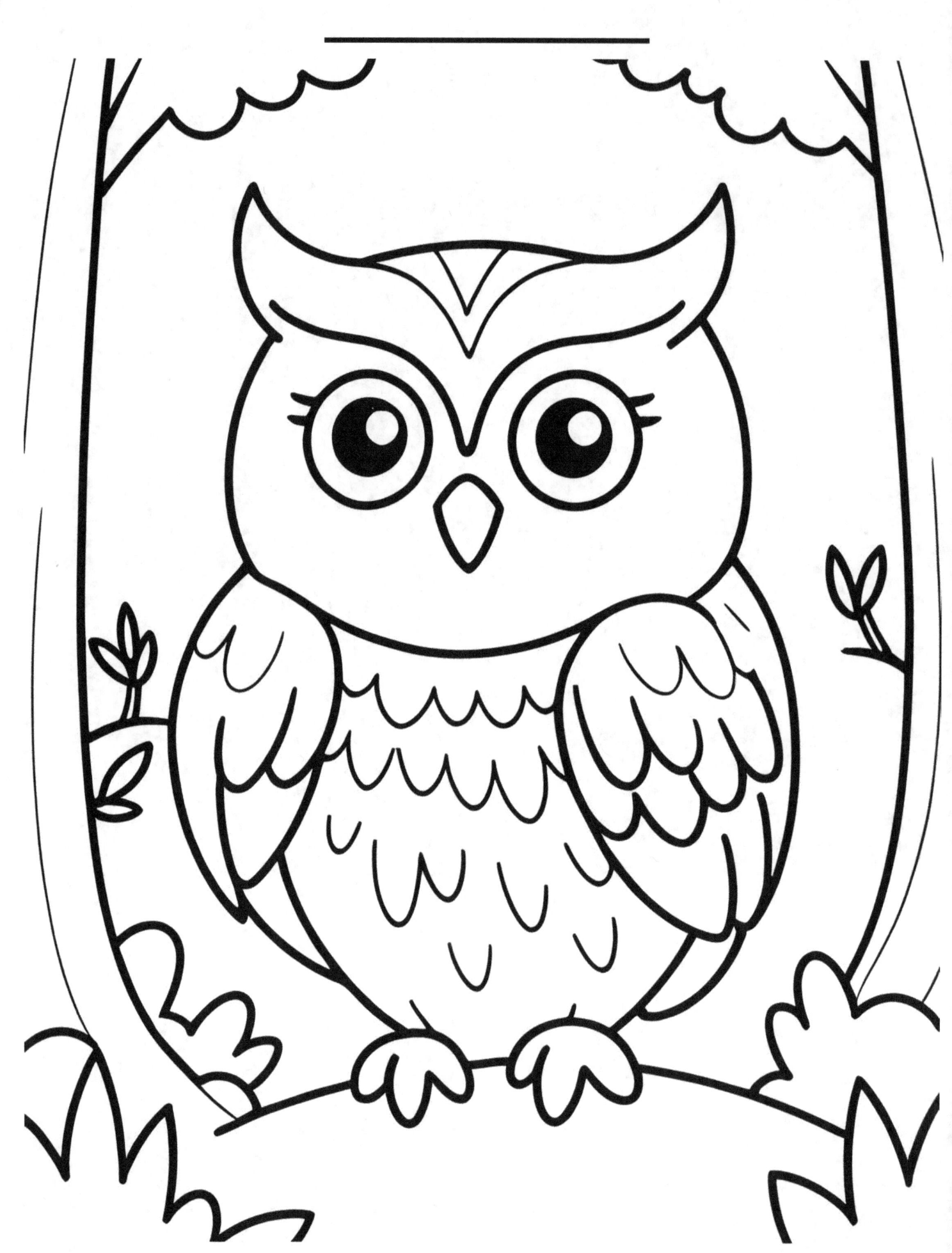

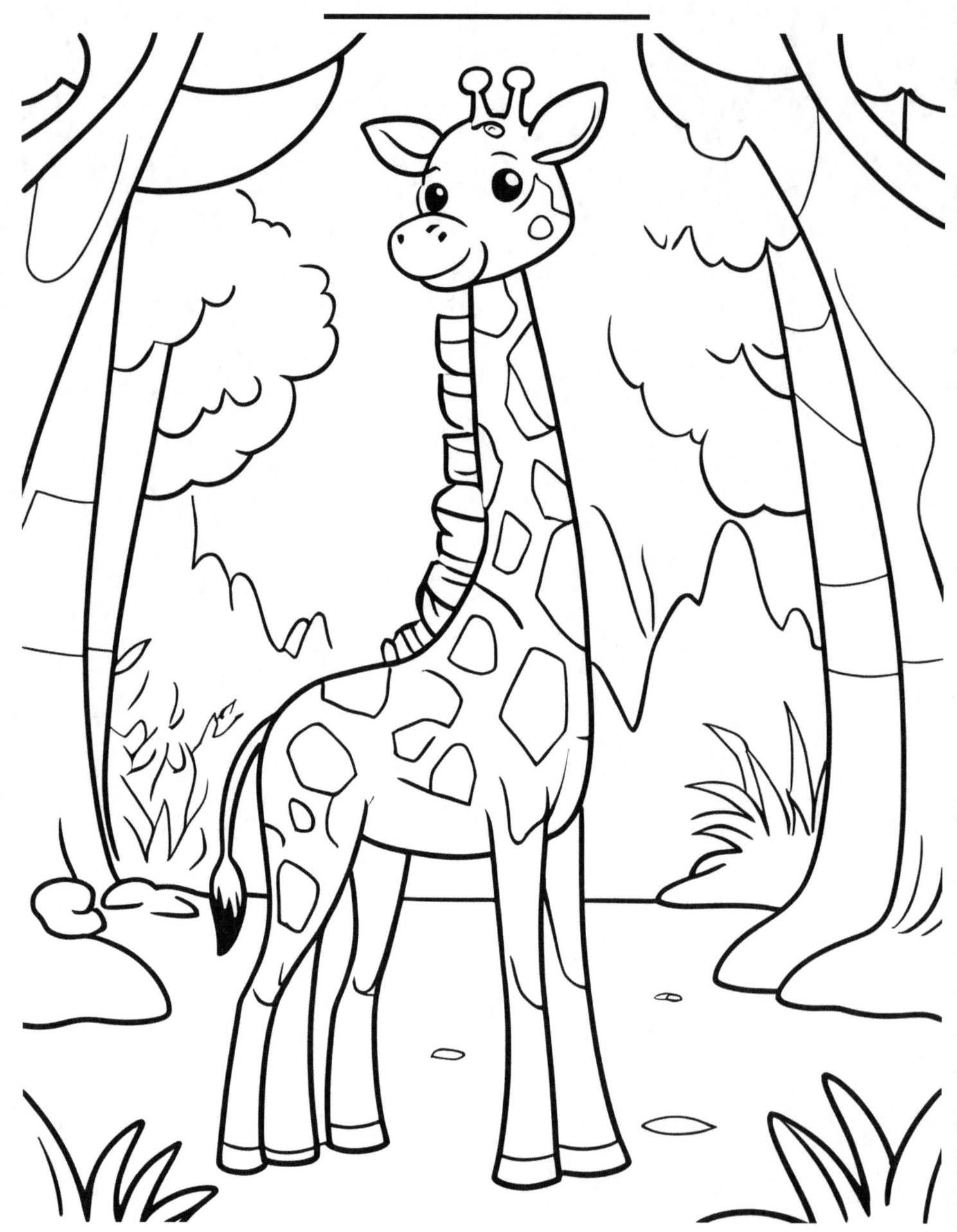

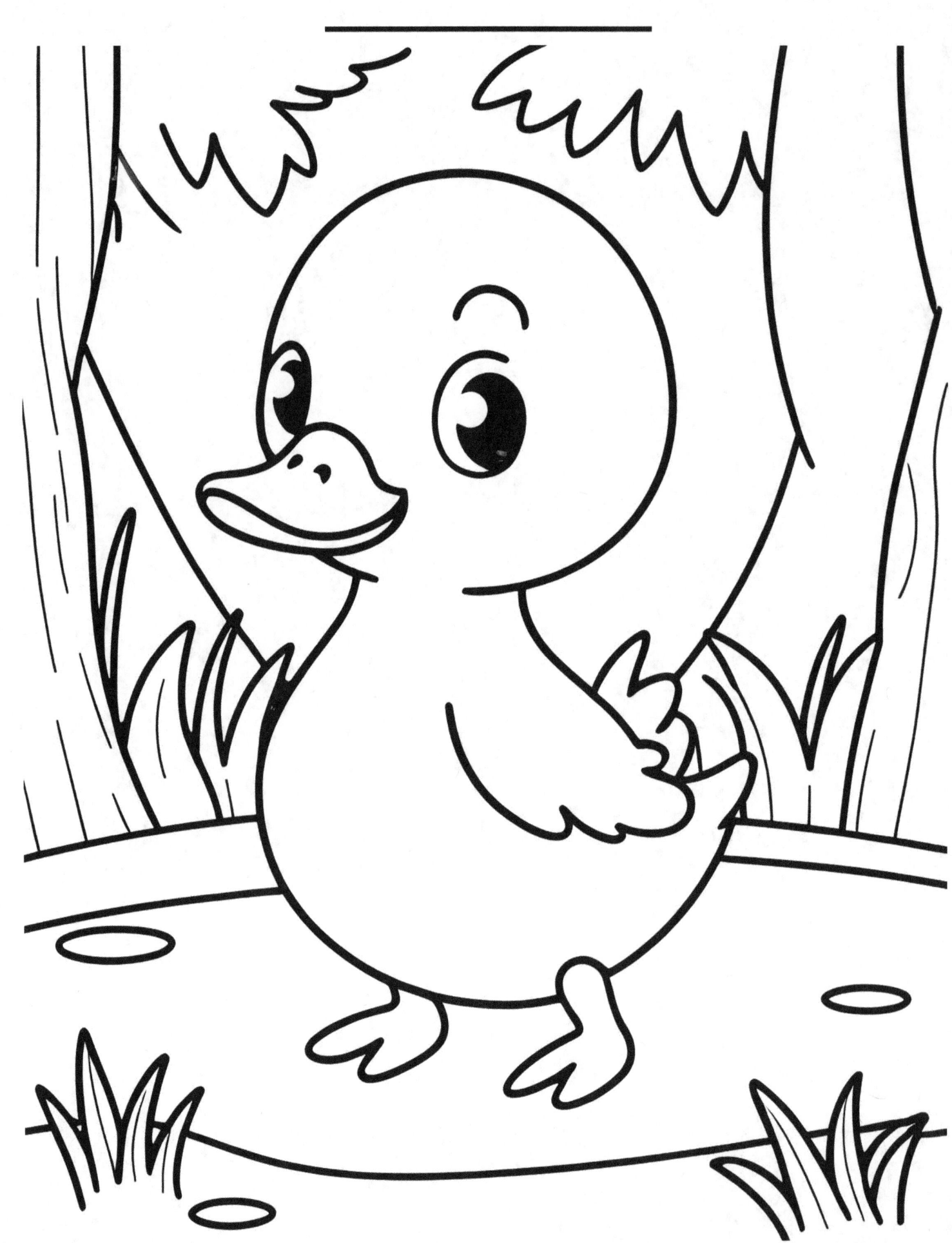

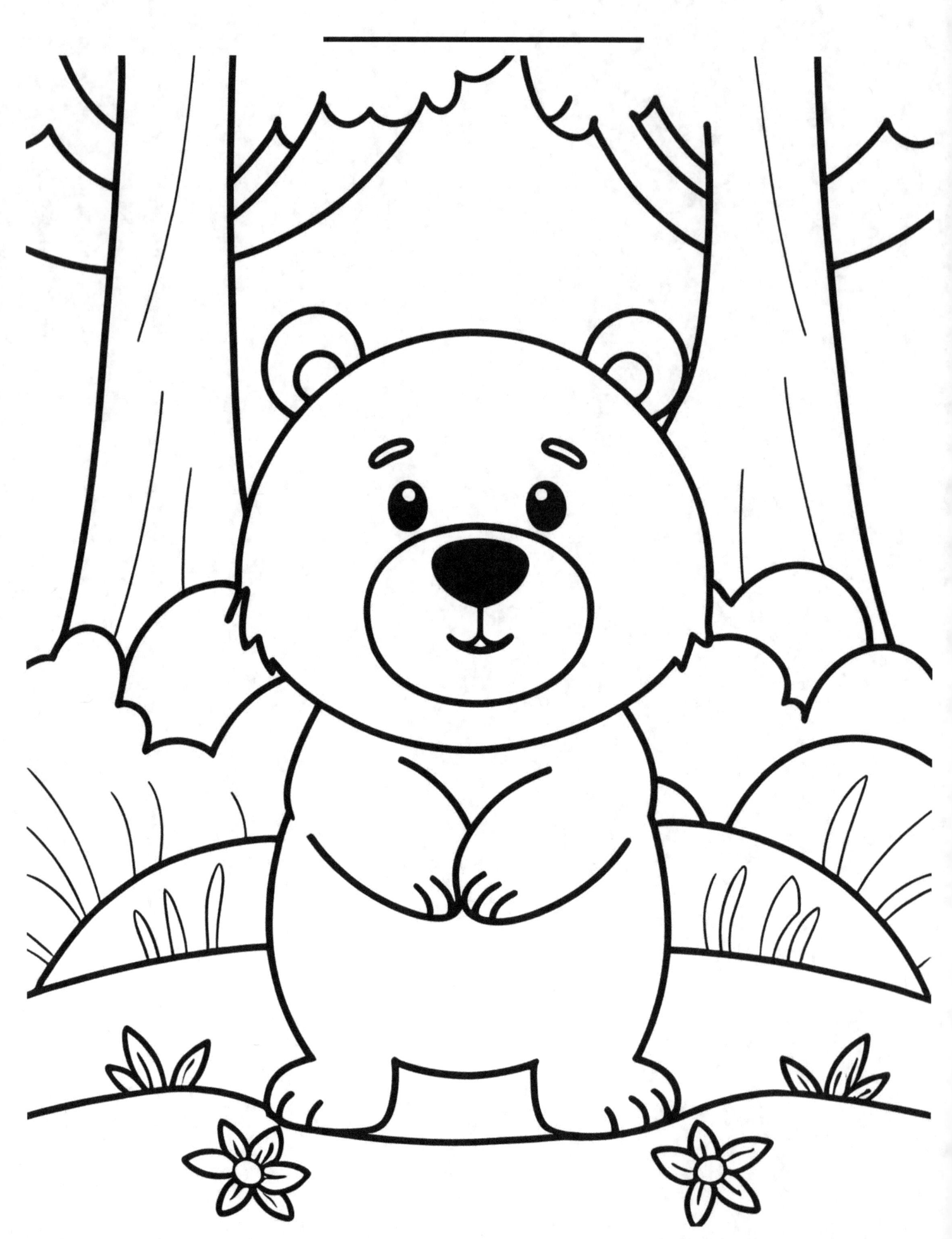

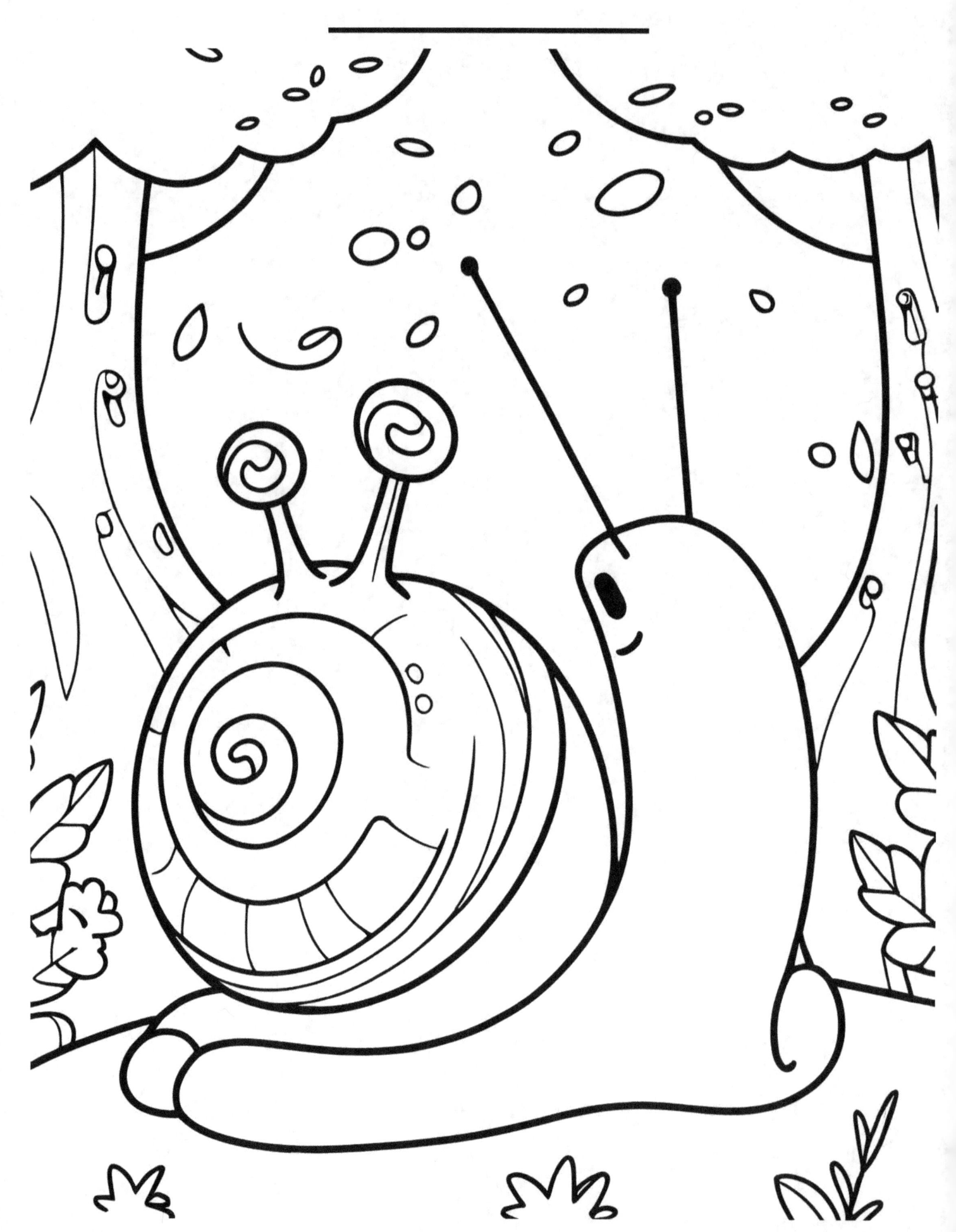

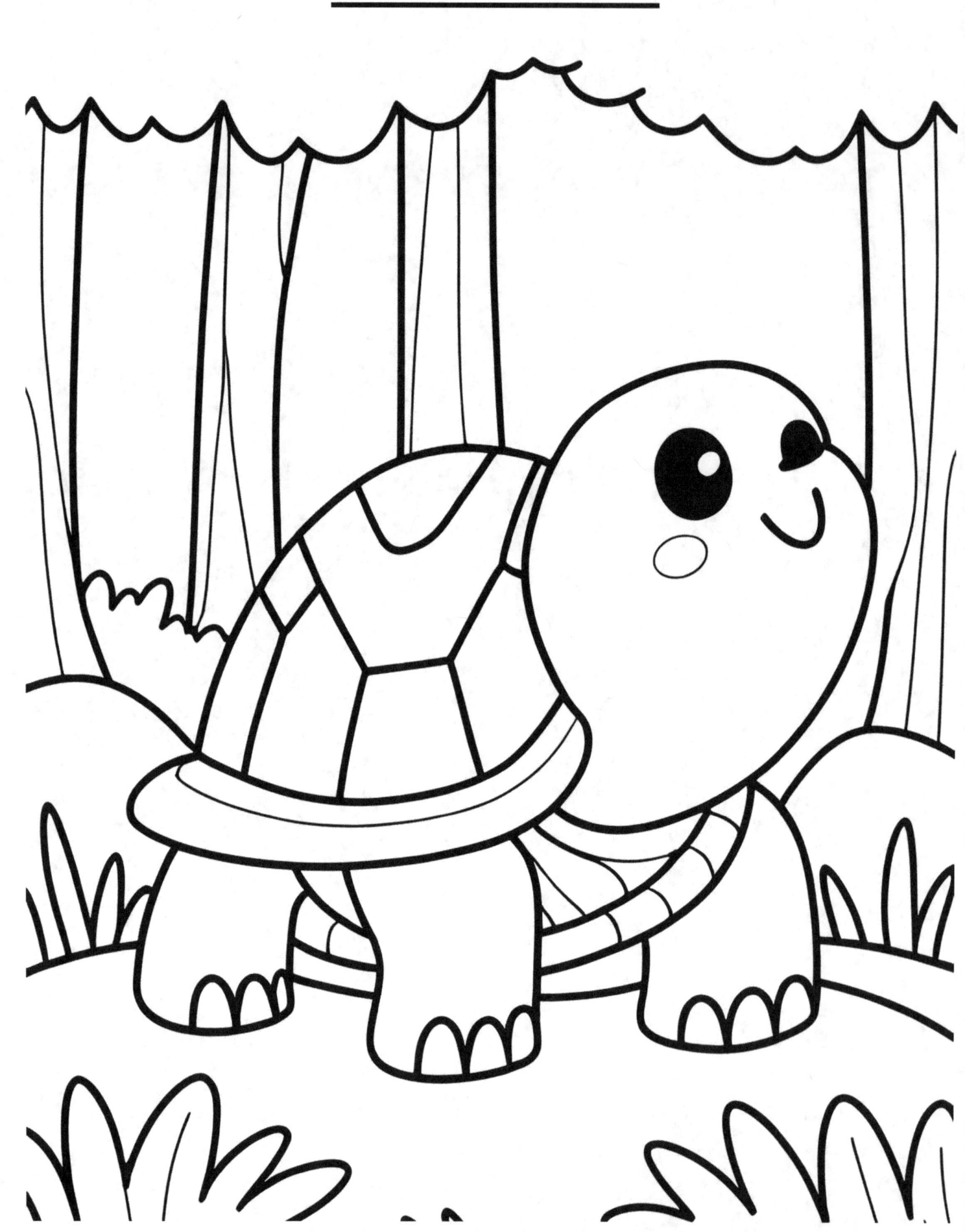

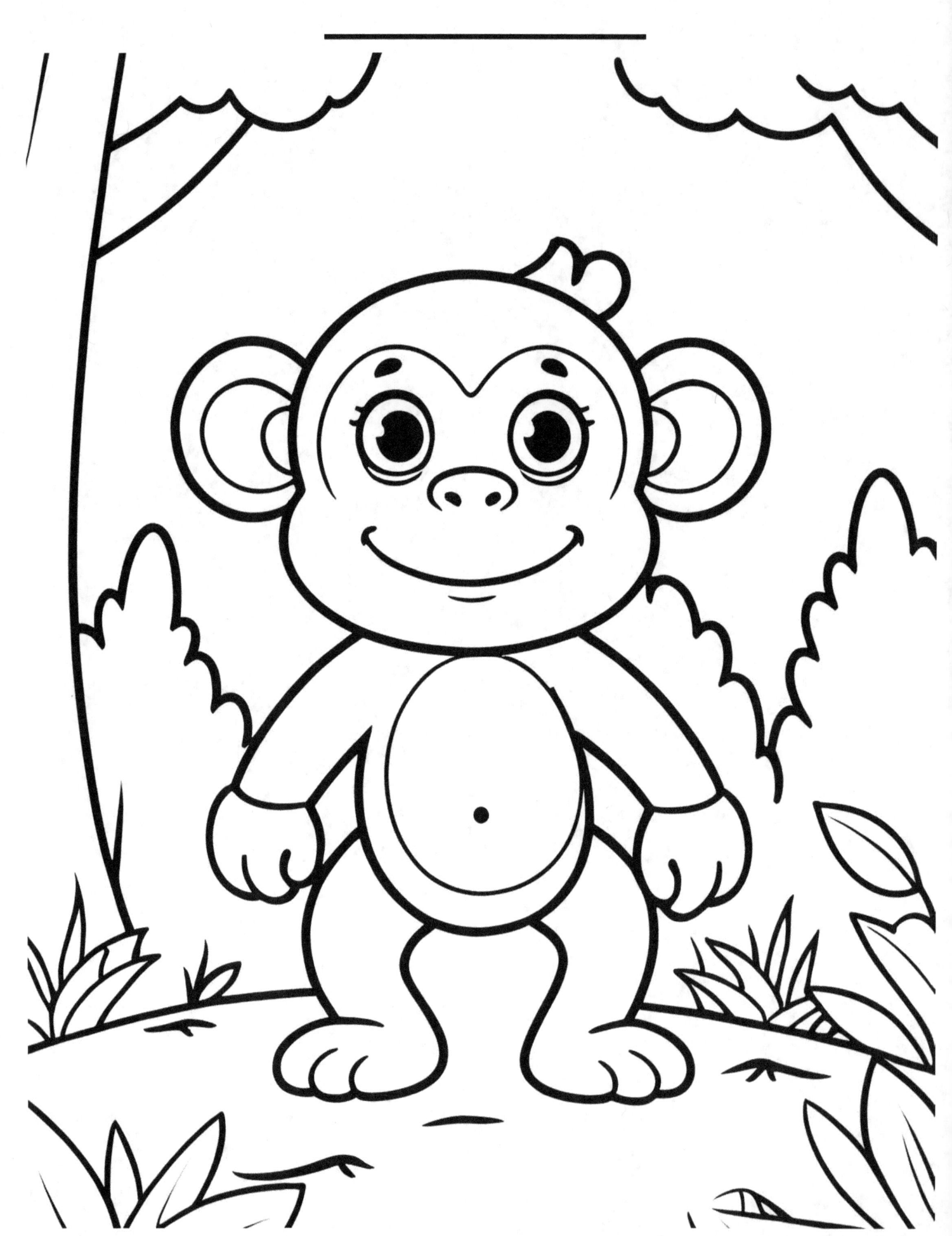

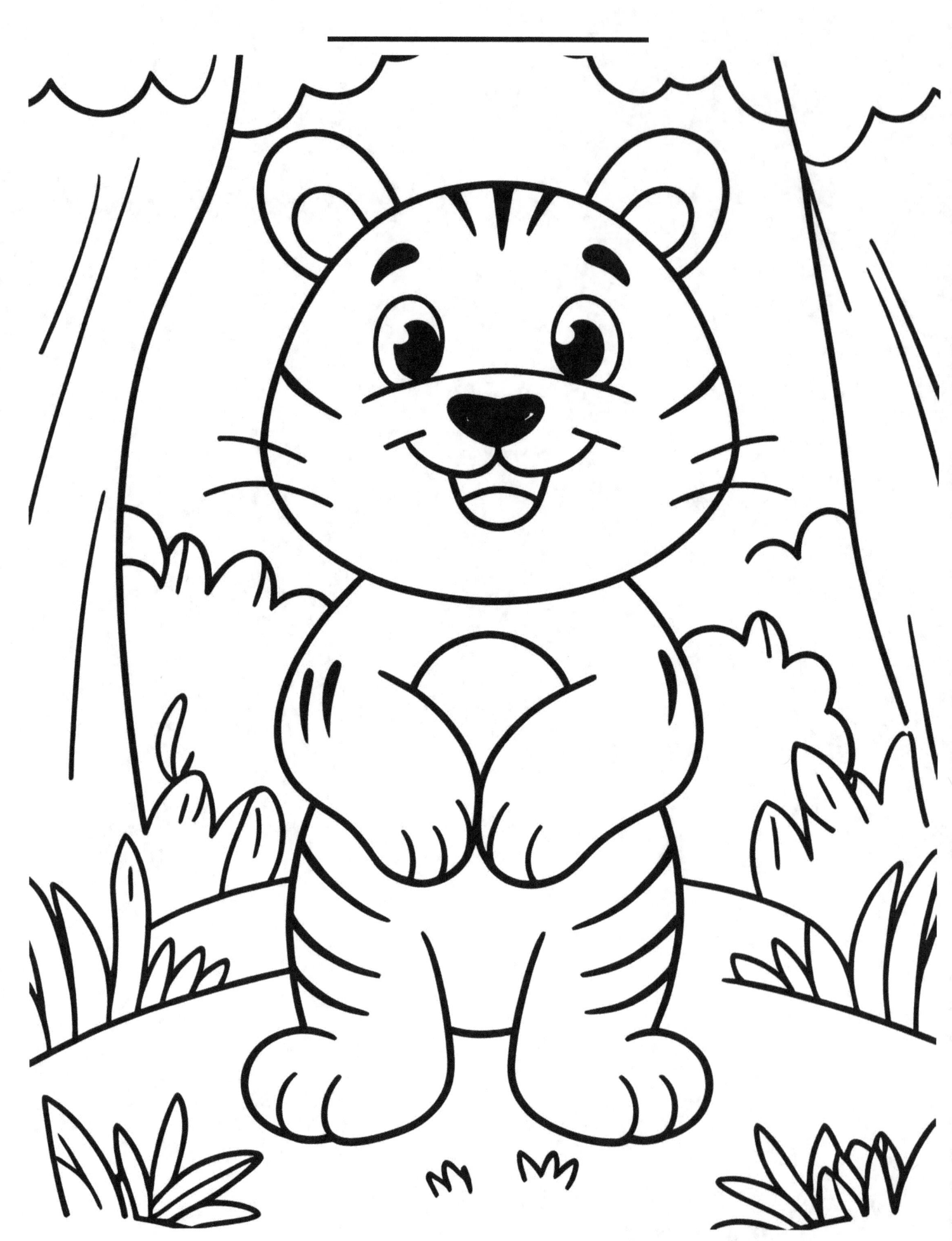

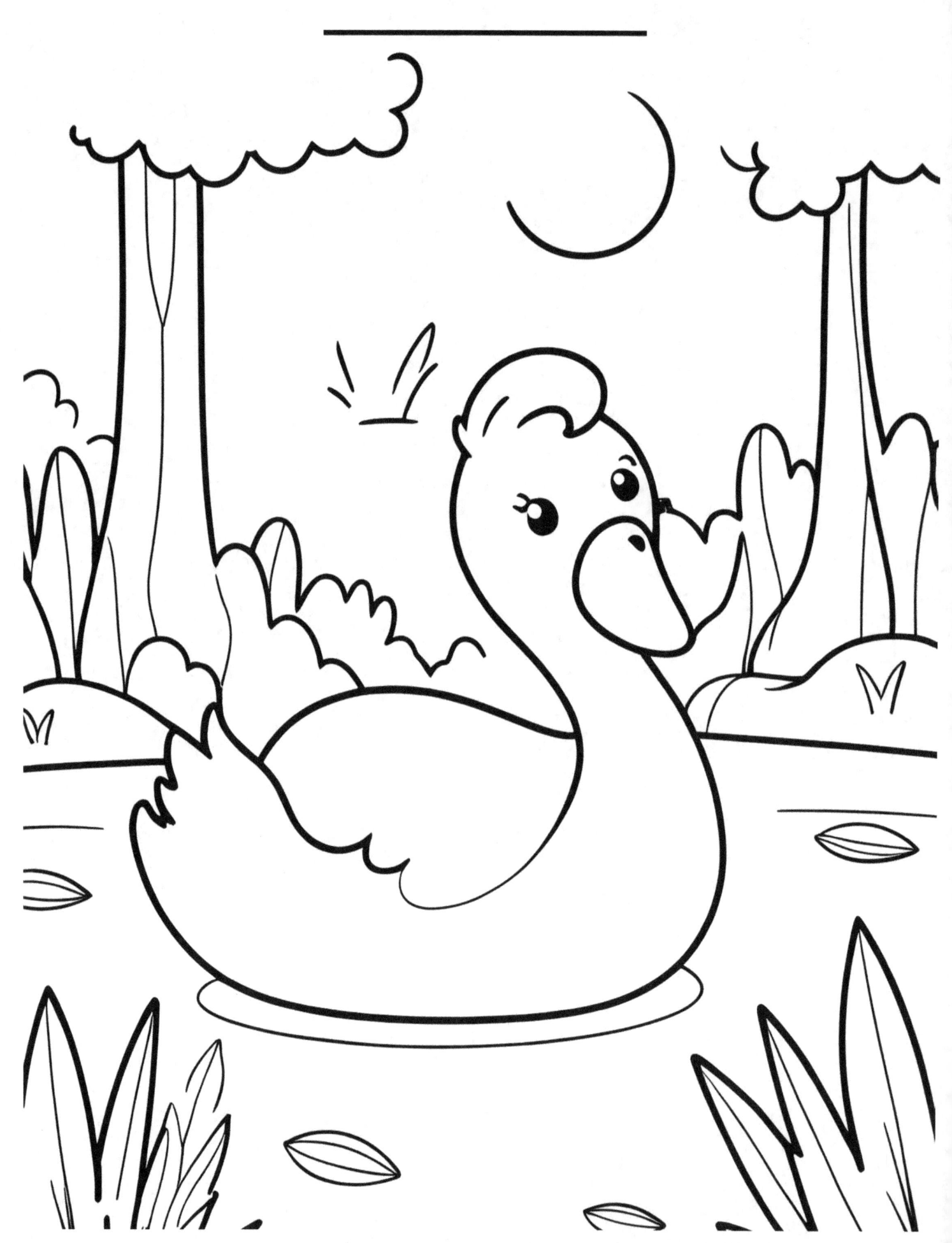

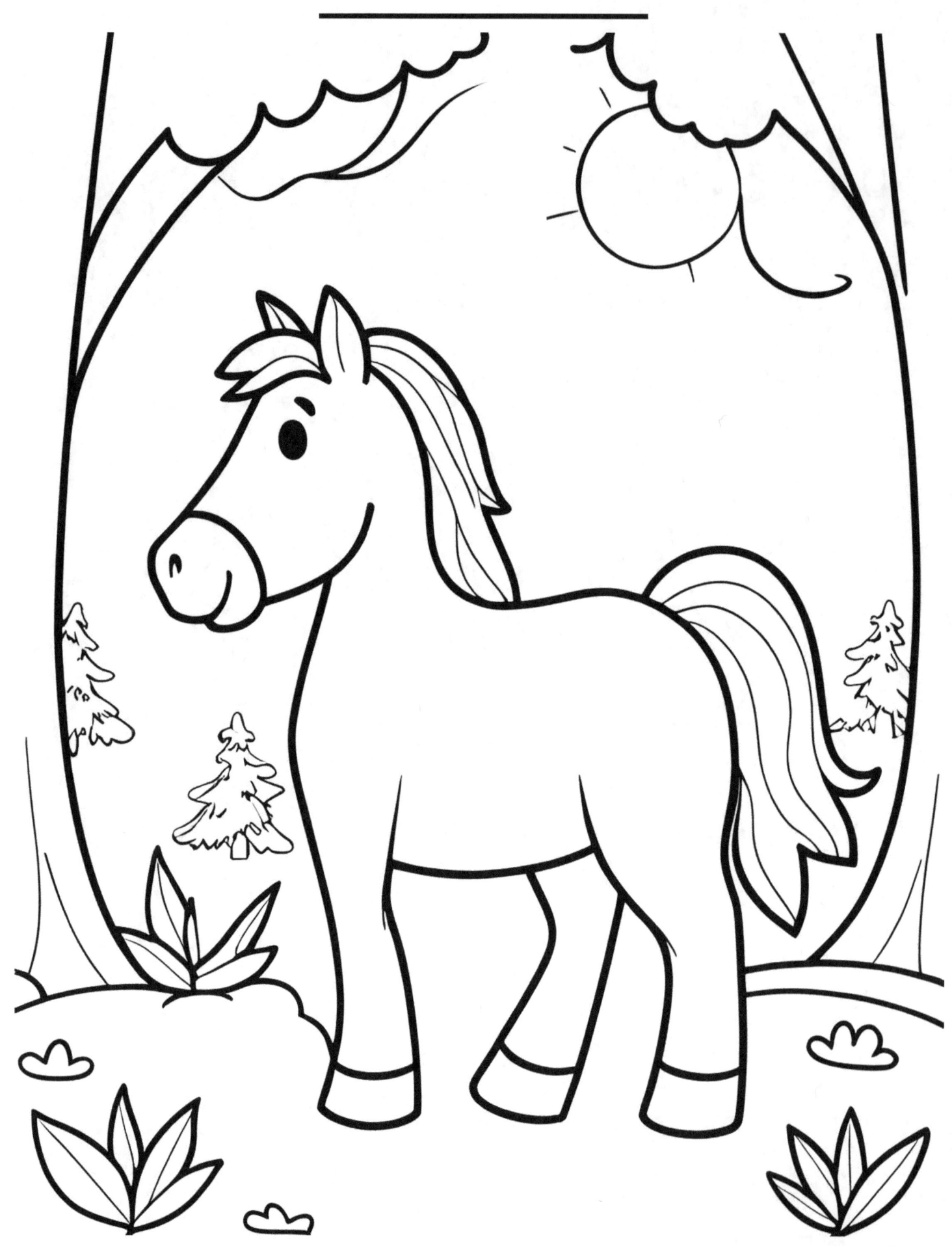

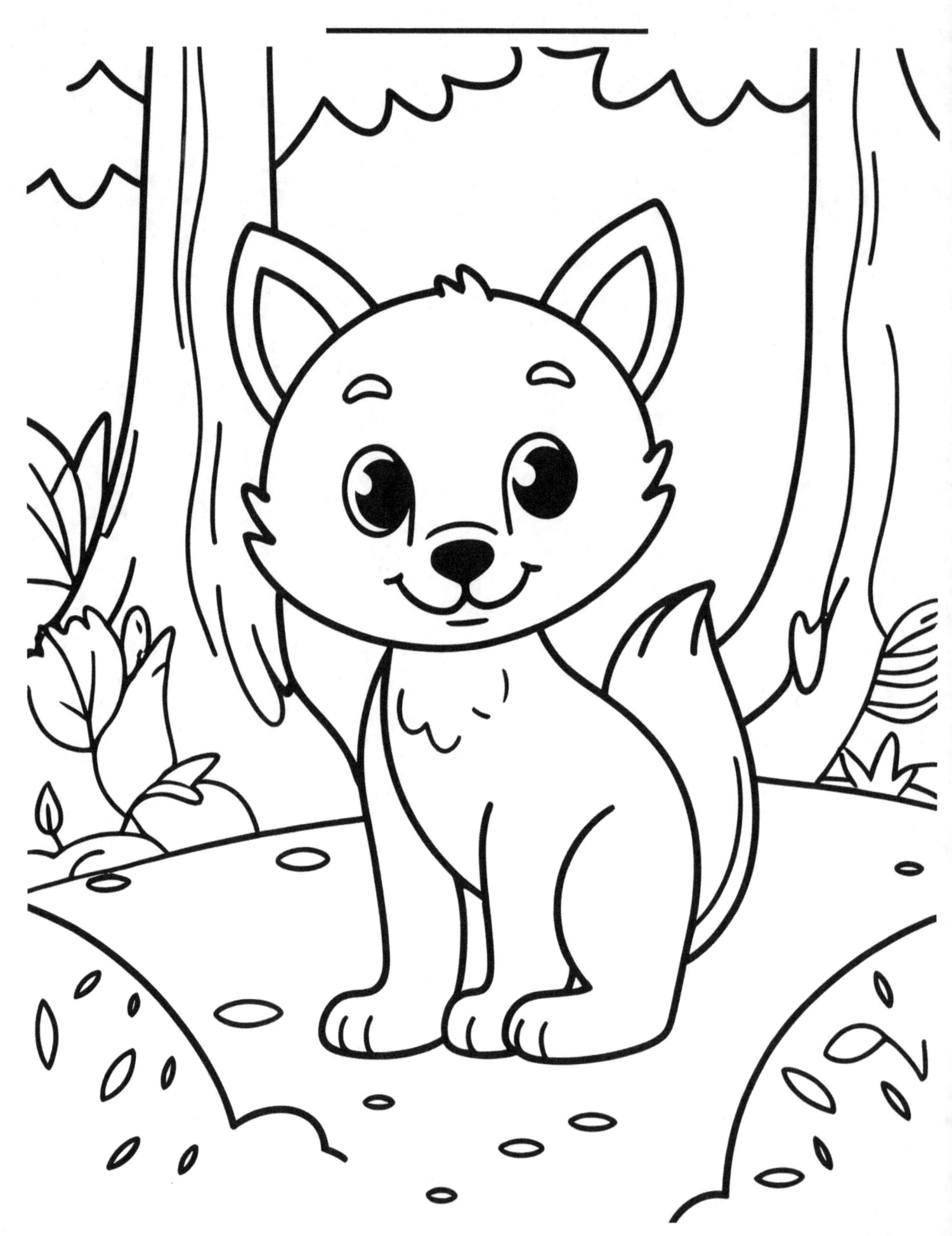

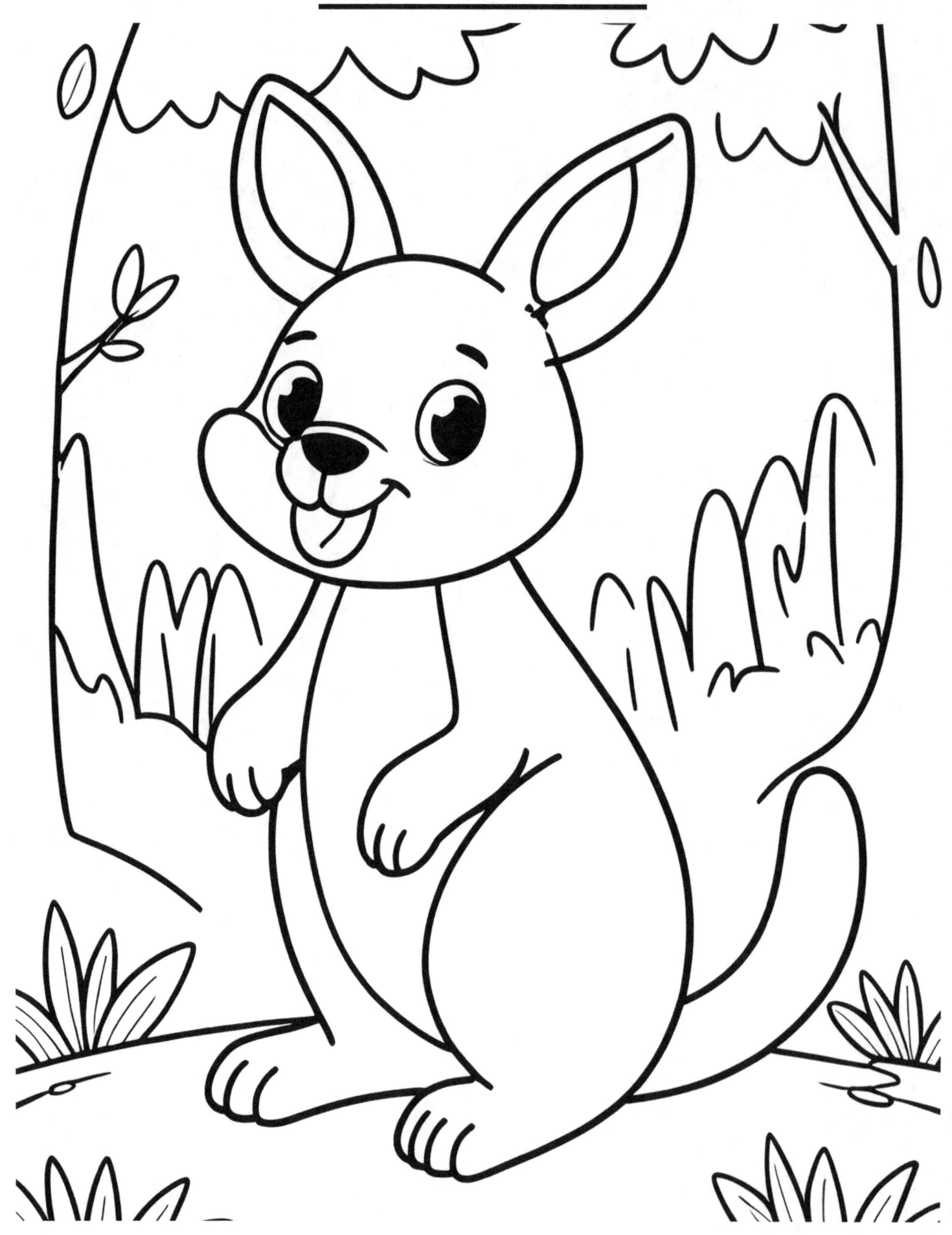

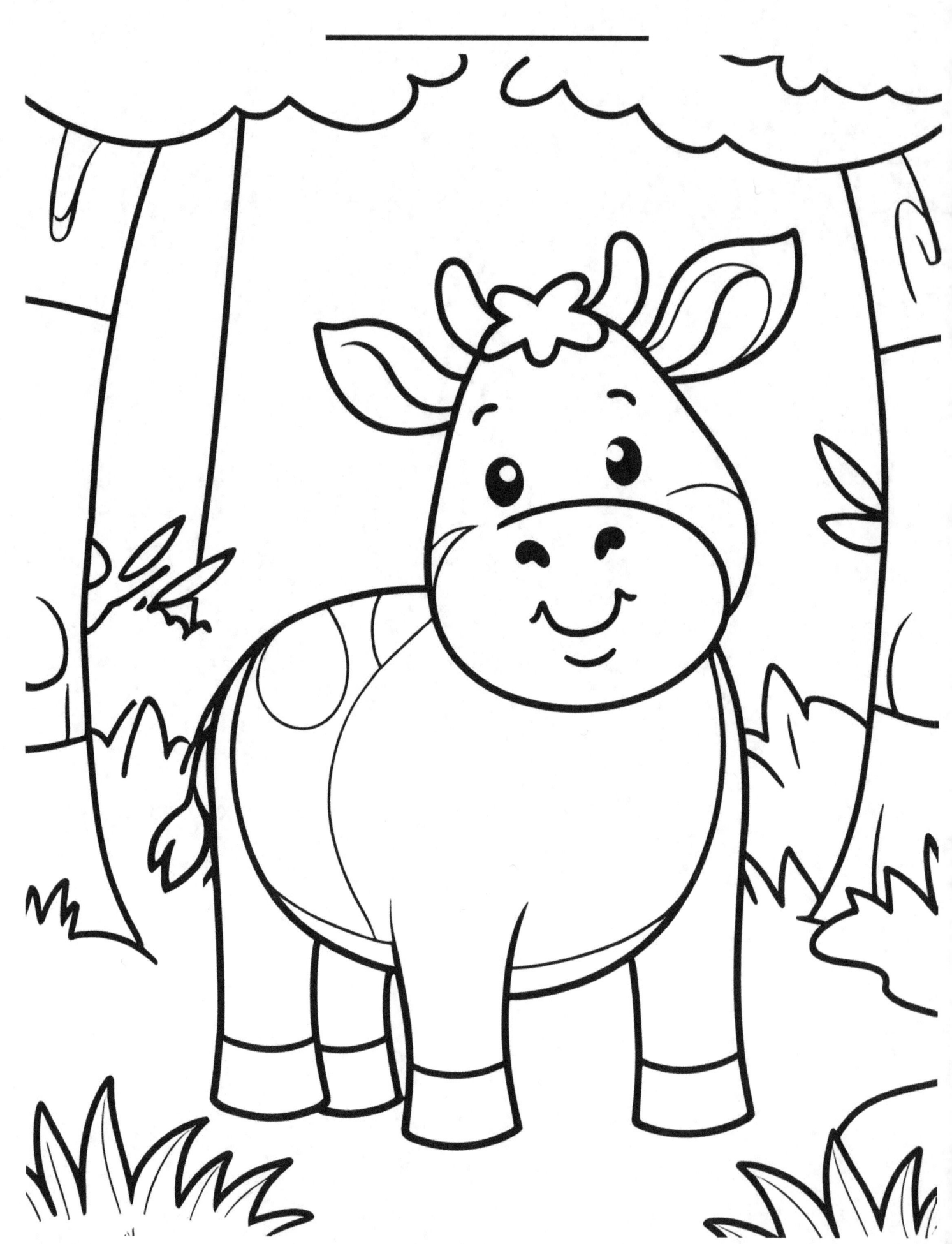

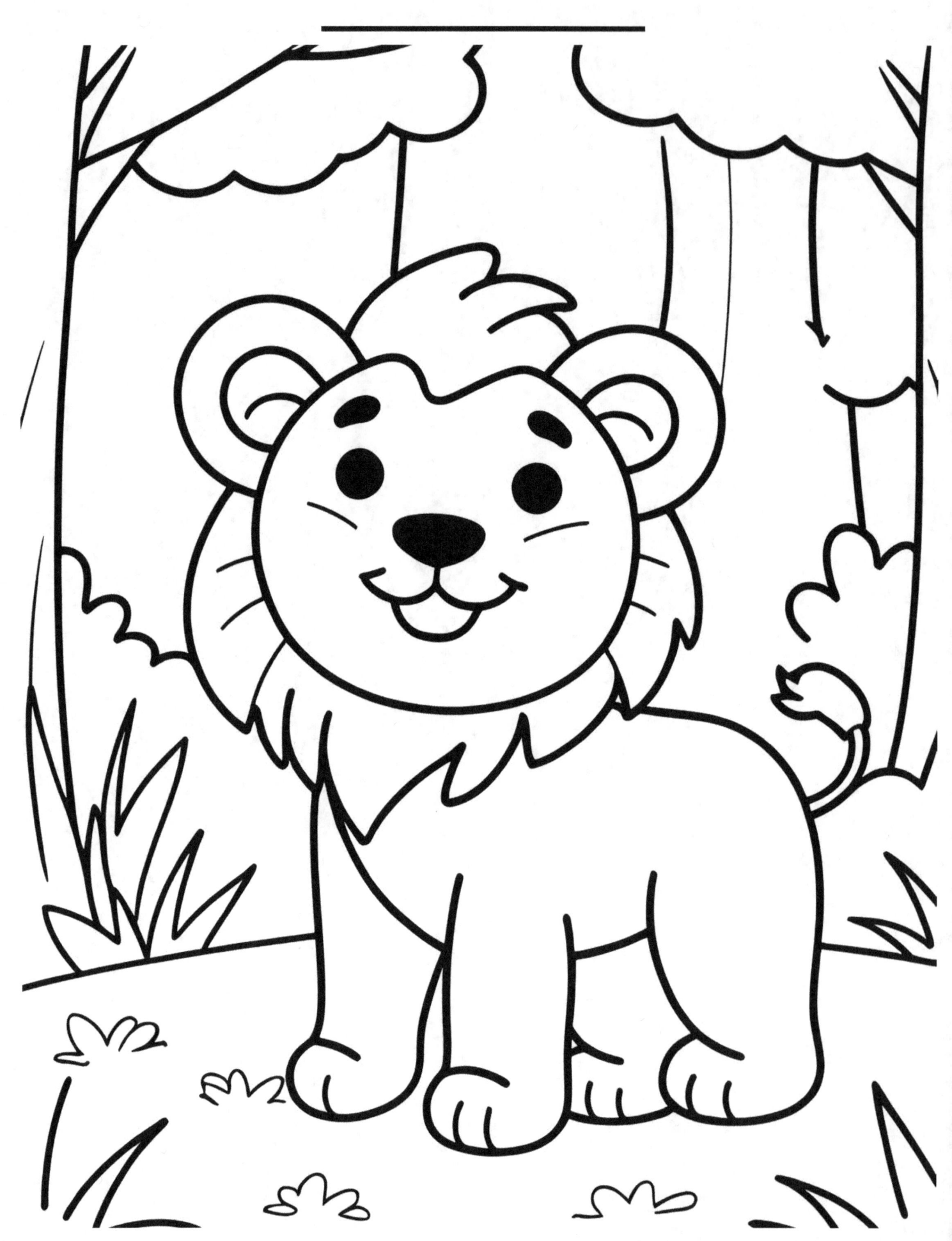

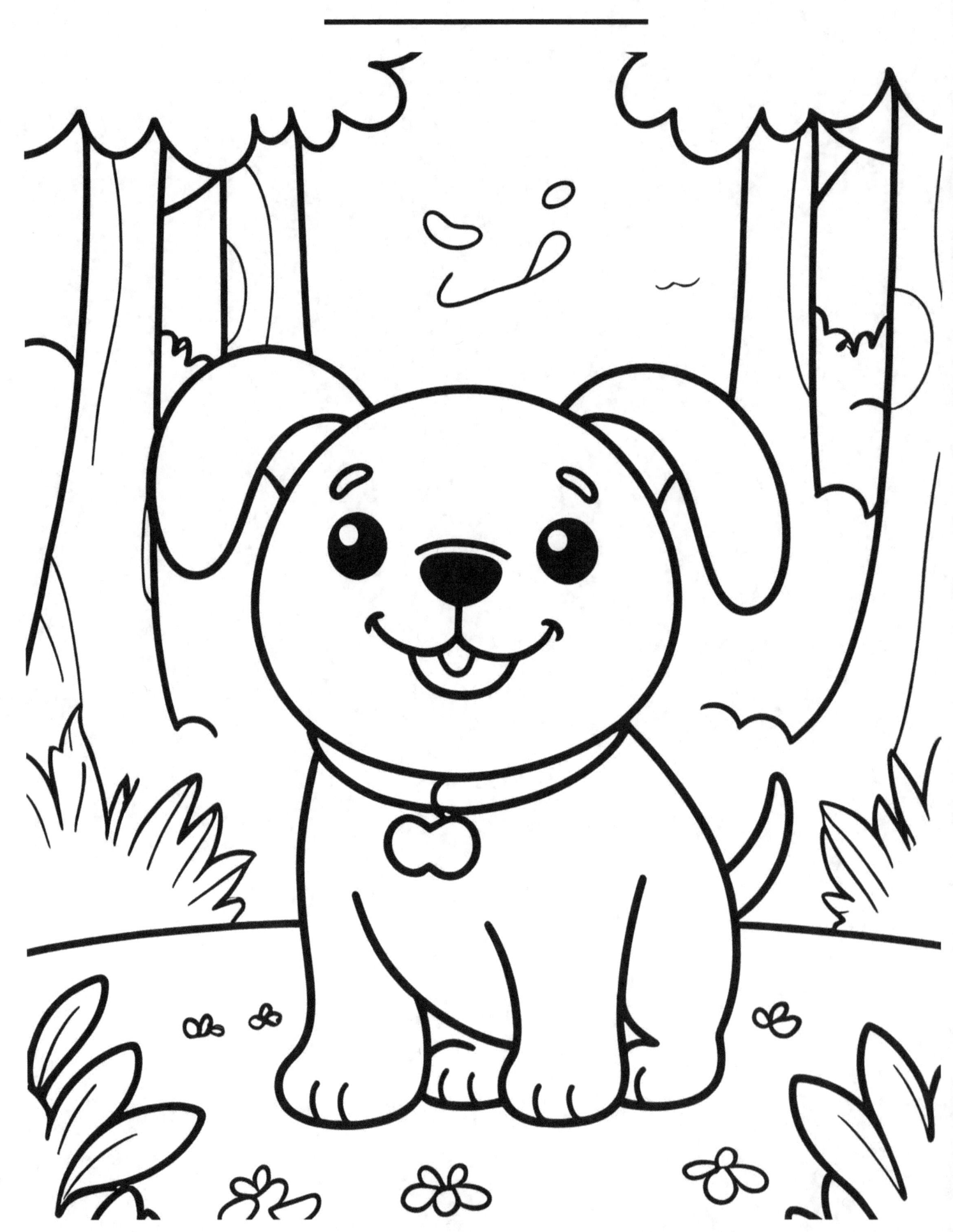

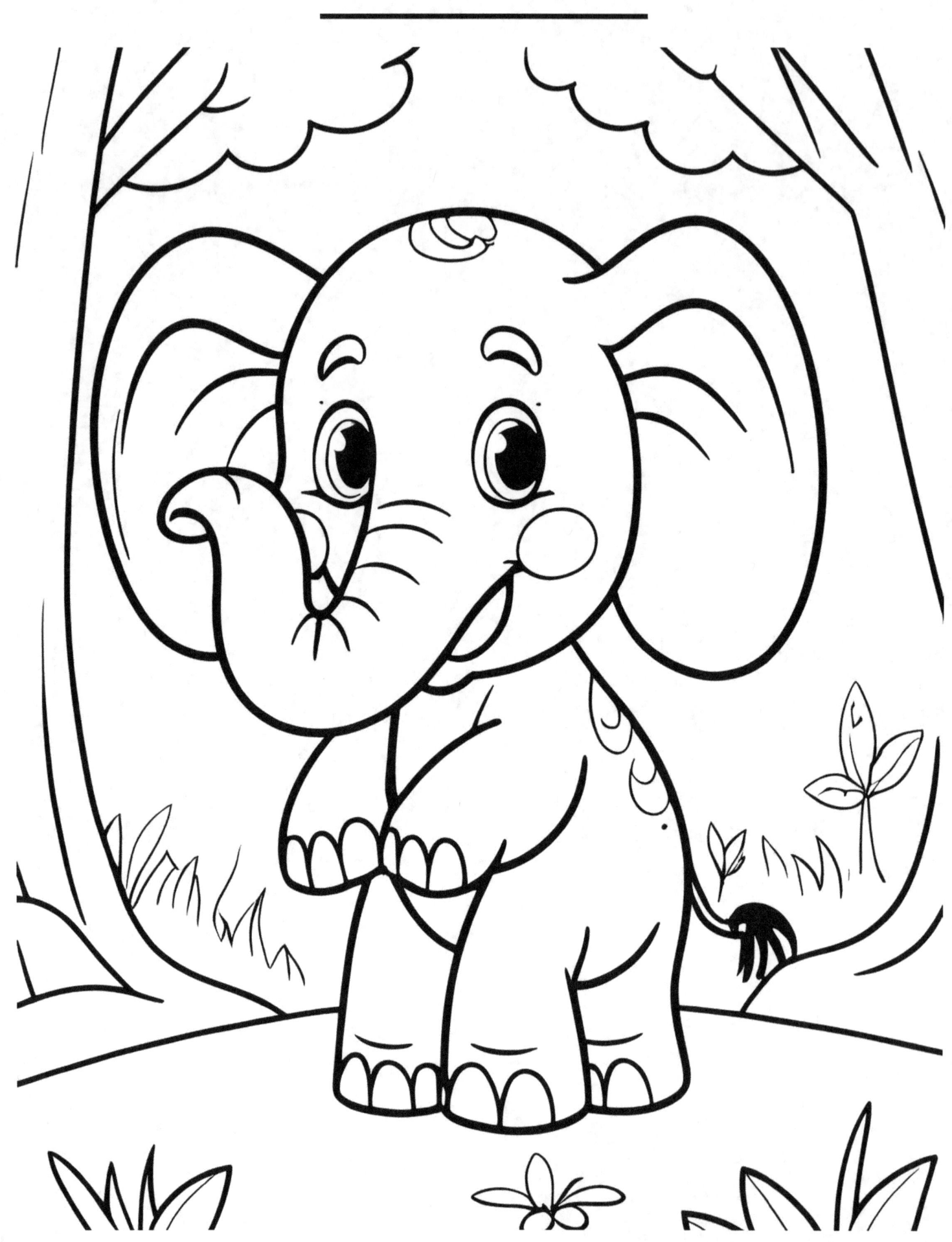

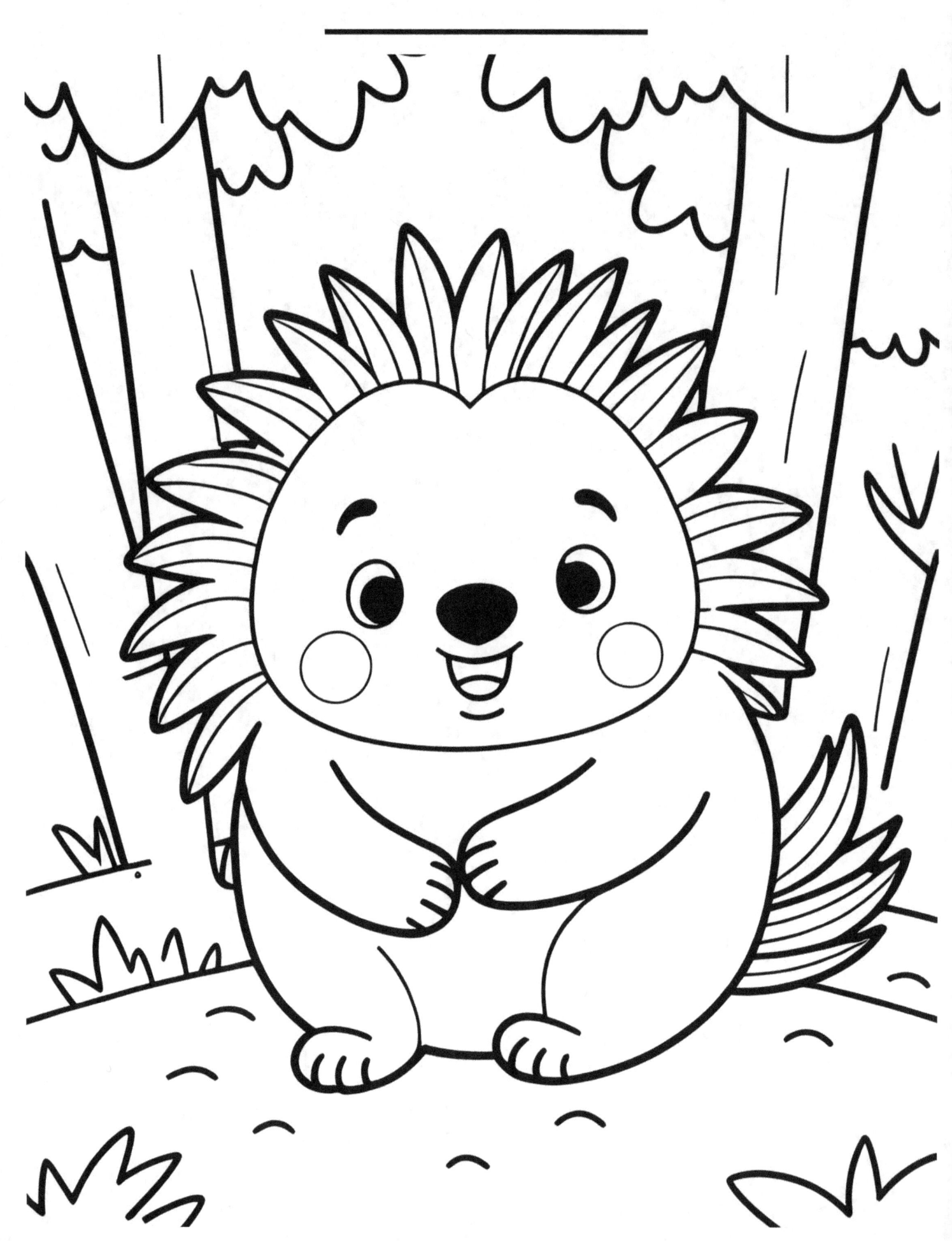

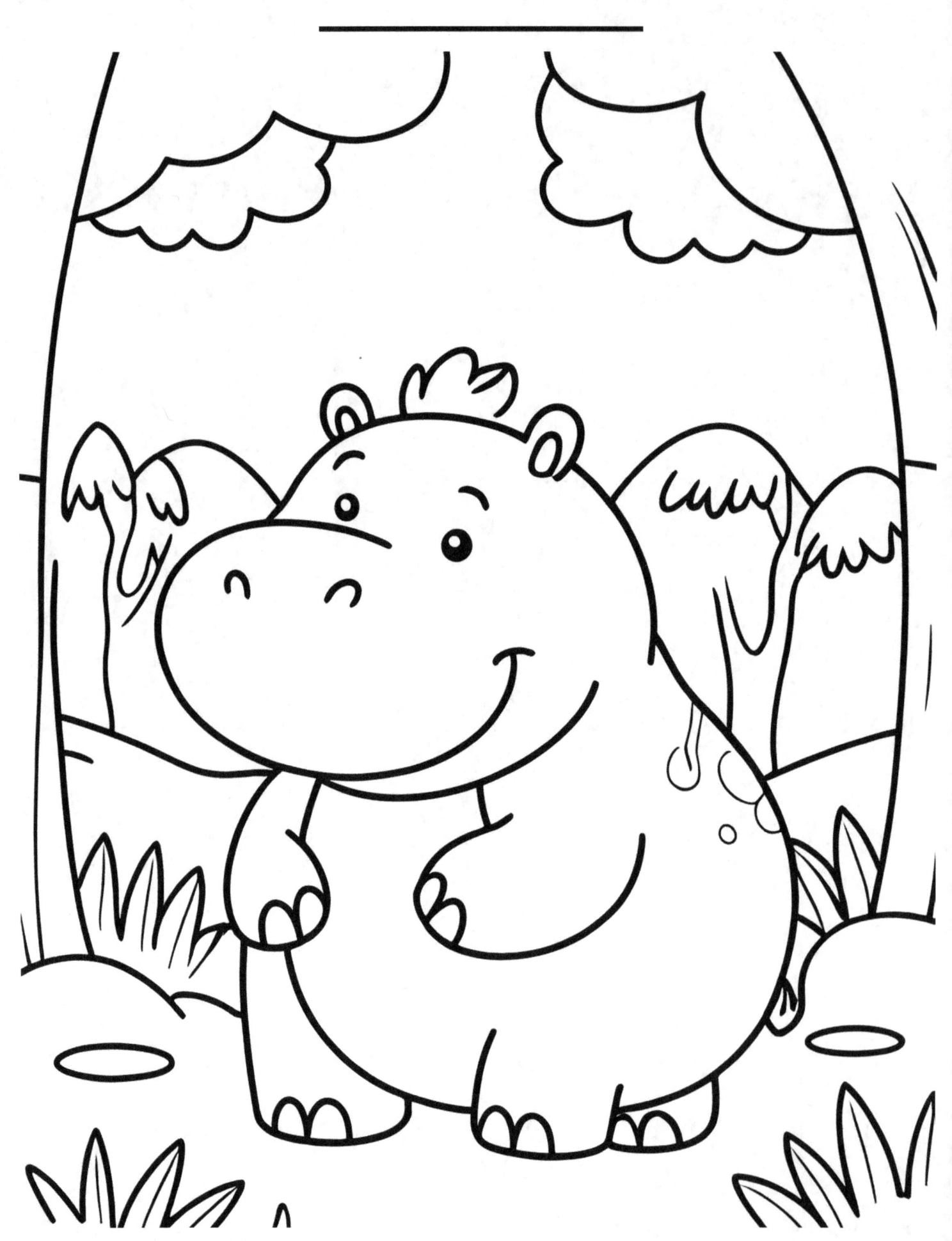

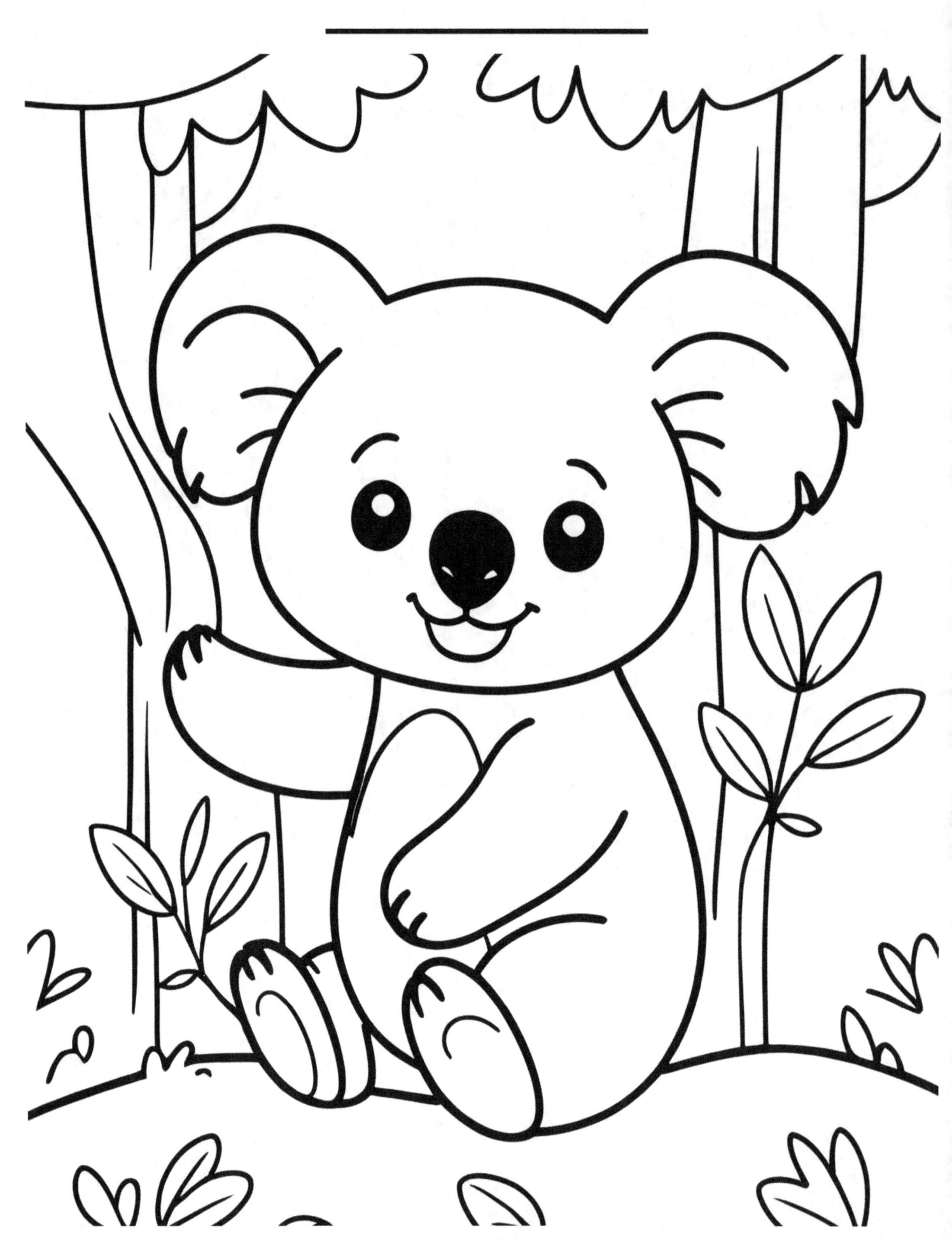

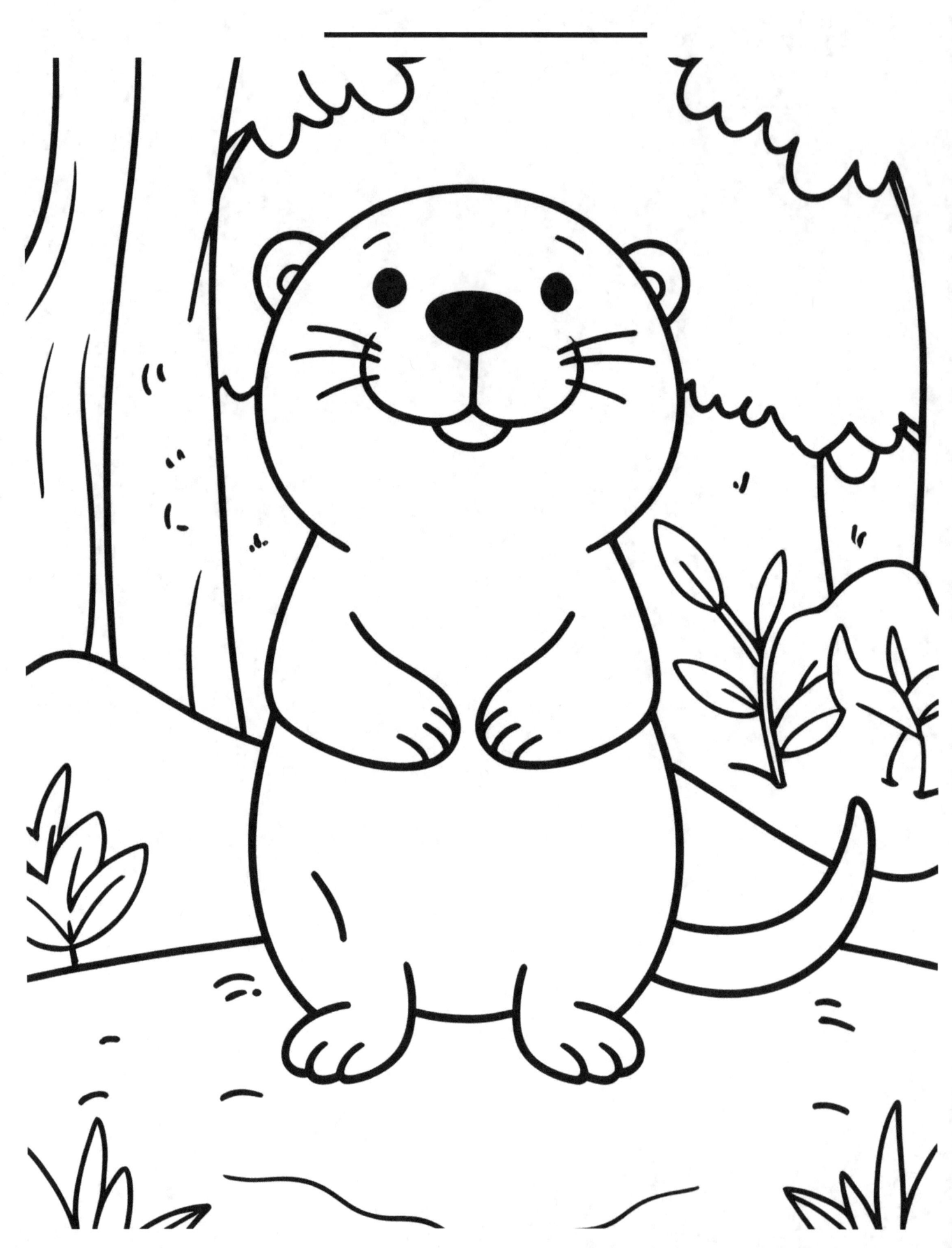

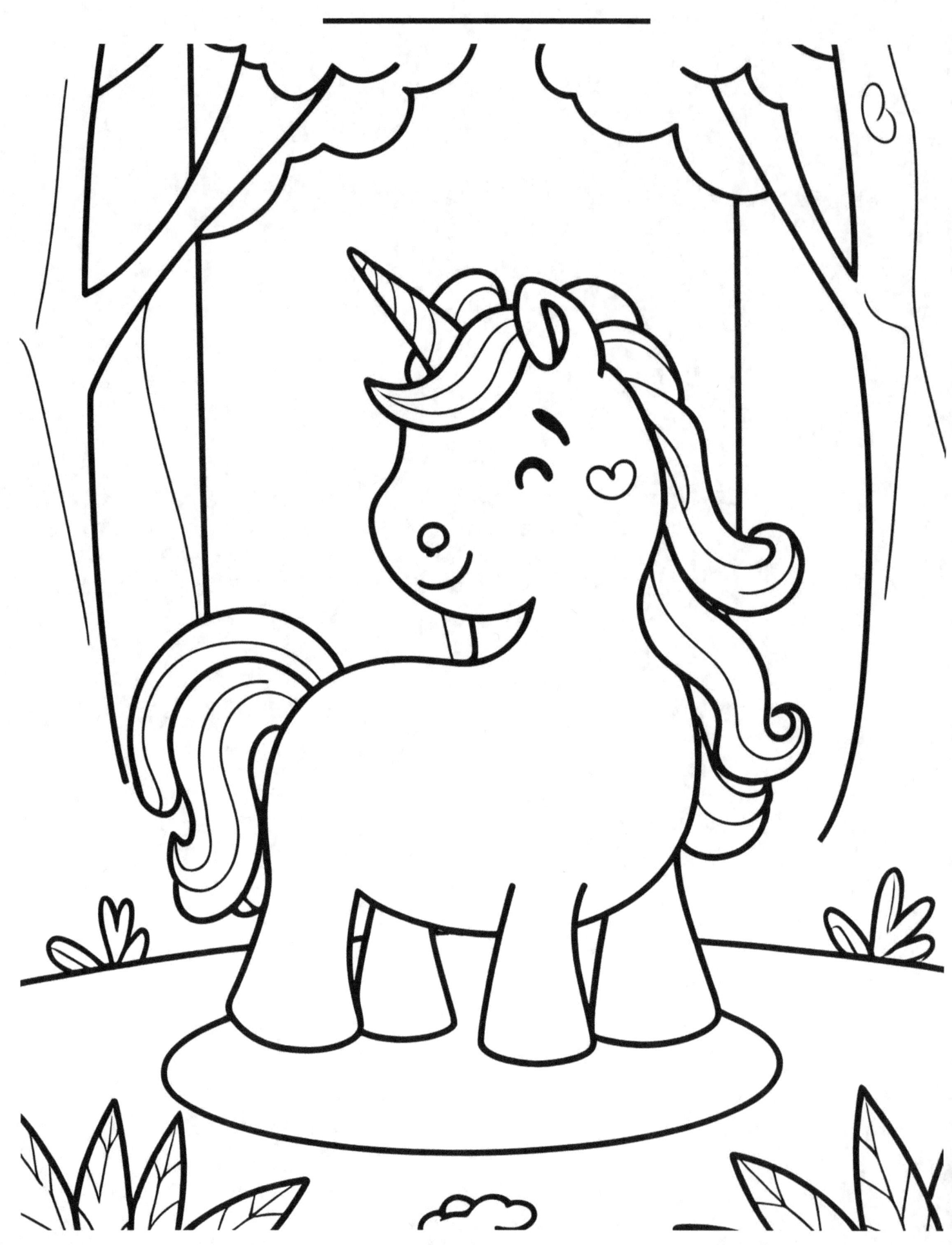

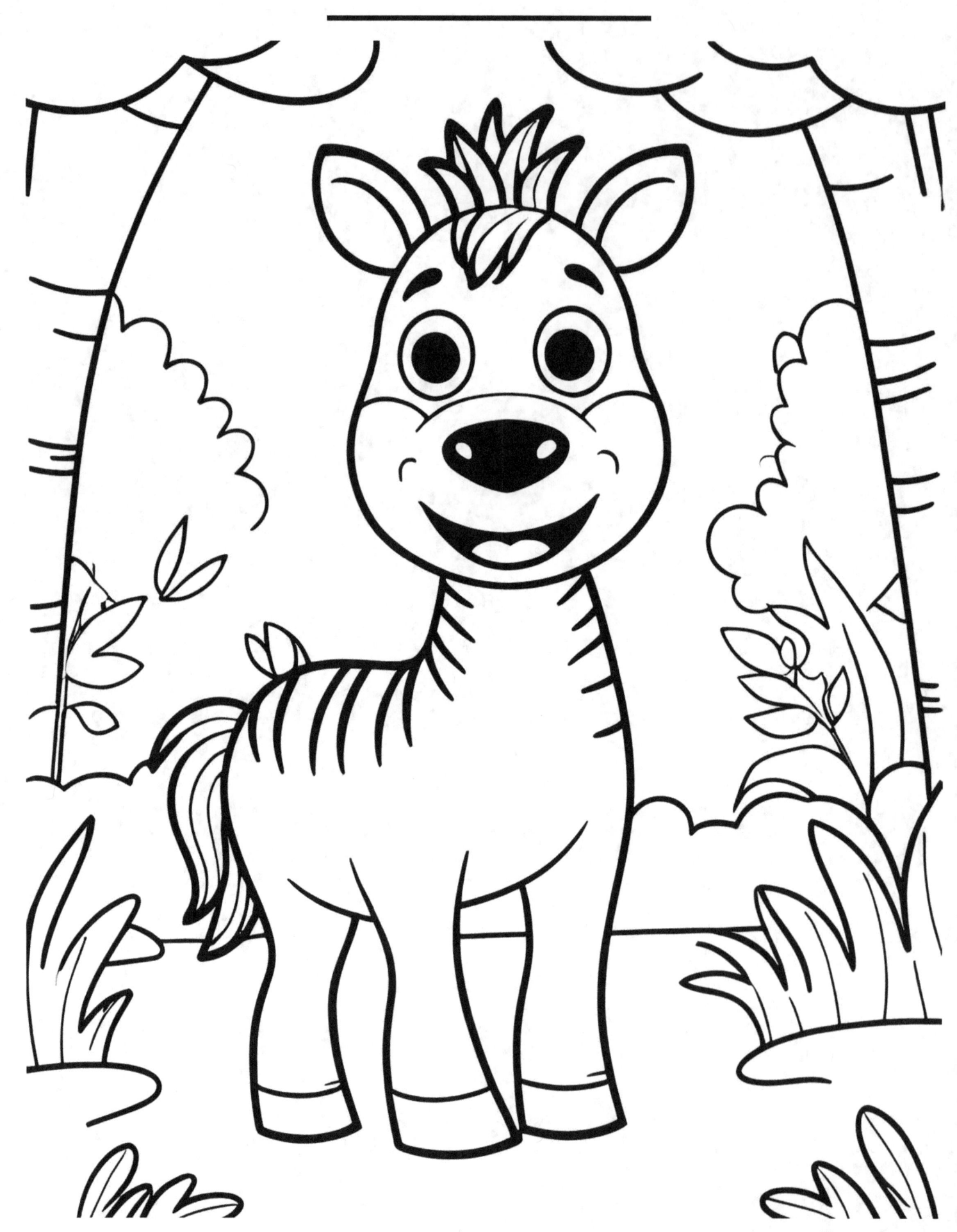

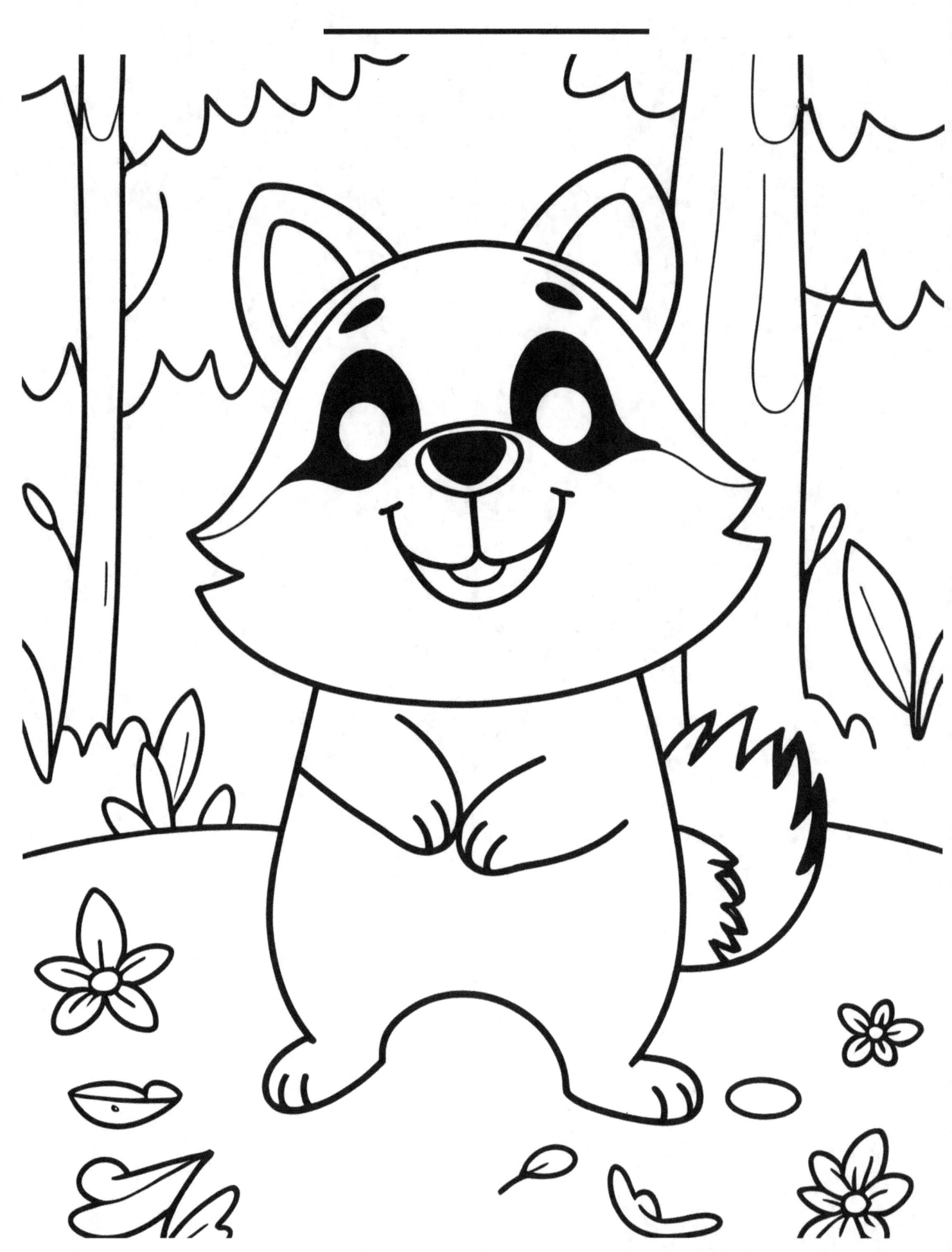

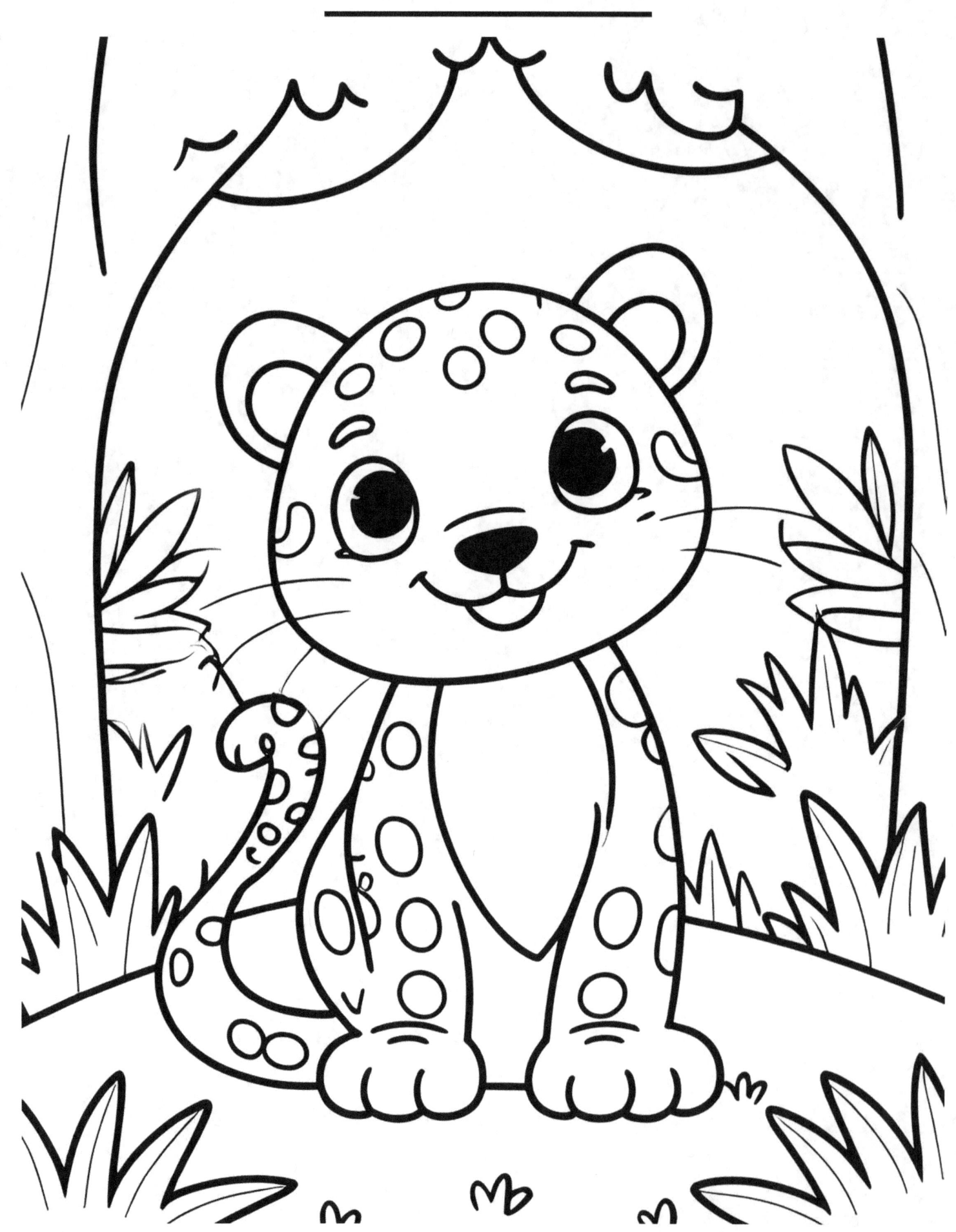

**At the end of the day, Mimo happily returned to his house planning his next adventure through the woods with his new friends.**

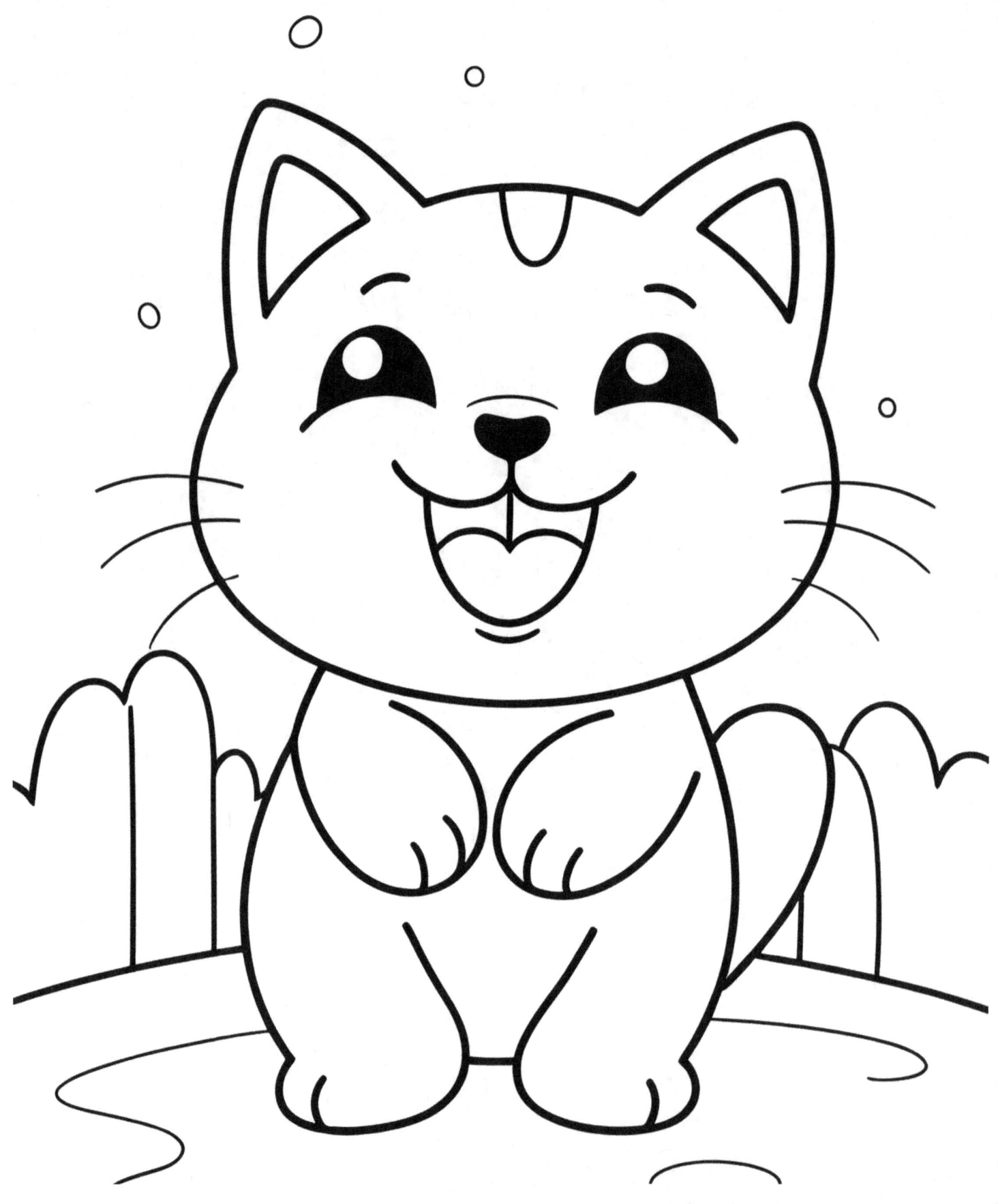